50 Shades of Stitches

Braids and Cables

Knitting Patterns
with Step-by-Step Instructions

Copyright © 2020 by SCR Media Inc. All rights reserved. This book or any portion thereof may not be reproduced or used in any manner whatsoever without the express written permission of the publisher except for the use of brief quotations in a book review.

Printed in the United States of America First Printing, 2020

ISBN 978-1-63227-3086

SCR MEDIA Inc Box 7103
Delray Beach Fl 33482
561-909-6975

If you like this book and found some benefit in reading it, I'd like to hear from you and hope that you could take some time to post a review on Amazon. Your feedback and support will help the author to greatly improve her writing craft for future projects and make this book even better. Just type this link into your web browser **Getbook.at/Vol3** *or scan QR code.*

Contents

Pattern 1 1

Pattern 2 4

Pattern 3 7

Pattern 4 9

Pattern 5 11

Pattern 6 13

Pattern 7 16

Pattern 8 19

Pattern 9 21

Pattern 10 23

Pattern 11 25

Pattern 12 28

Pattern 13 30

Pattern 14 33

Pattern 15 35

Pattern 16 38

Pattern 17 40

Pattern 18 42

Pattern 19 44

Pattern 20 46

Pattern 21 48

Pattern 22 50

Pattern 23 52

Pattern 24 55

Pattern 25 57

Pattern 26 59

Pattern 27 61

Pattern 28 63

Pattern 29 66

Pattern 30 68

Pattern 31 70

Pattern 32 72

Pattern 33 74

Pattern 34 76

Pattern 35 78

Pattern 36 80

Pattern 37 83

Pattern 38 86

Pattern 39 88

Pattern 40 91

Pattern 41 93

Pattern 42 95

Pattern 43 97

Pattern 44 99

Pattern 45 102

Pattern 46 104

Pattern 47 106

Pattern 48 109

Pattern 49 113

Pattern 50. 115

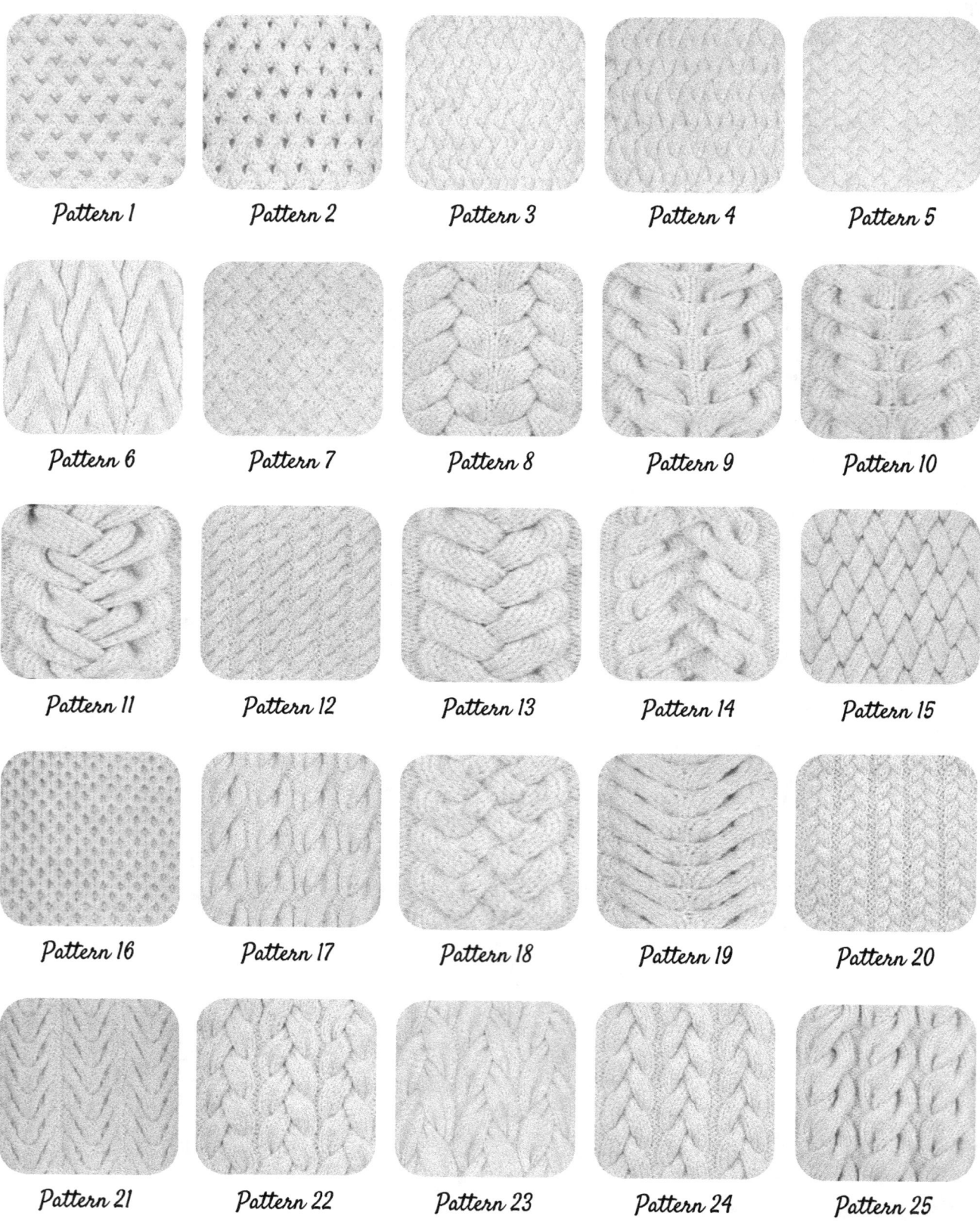

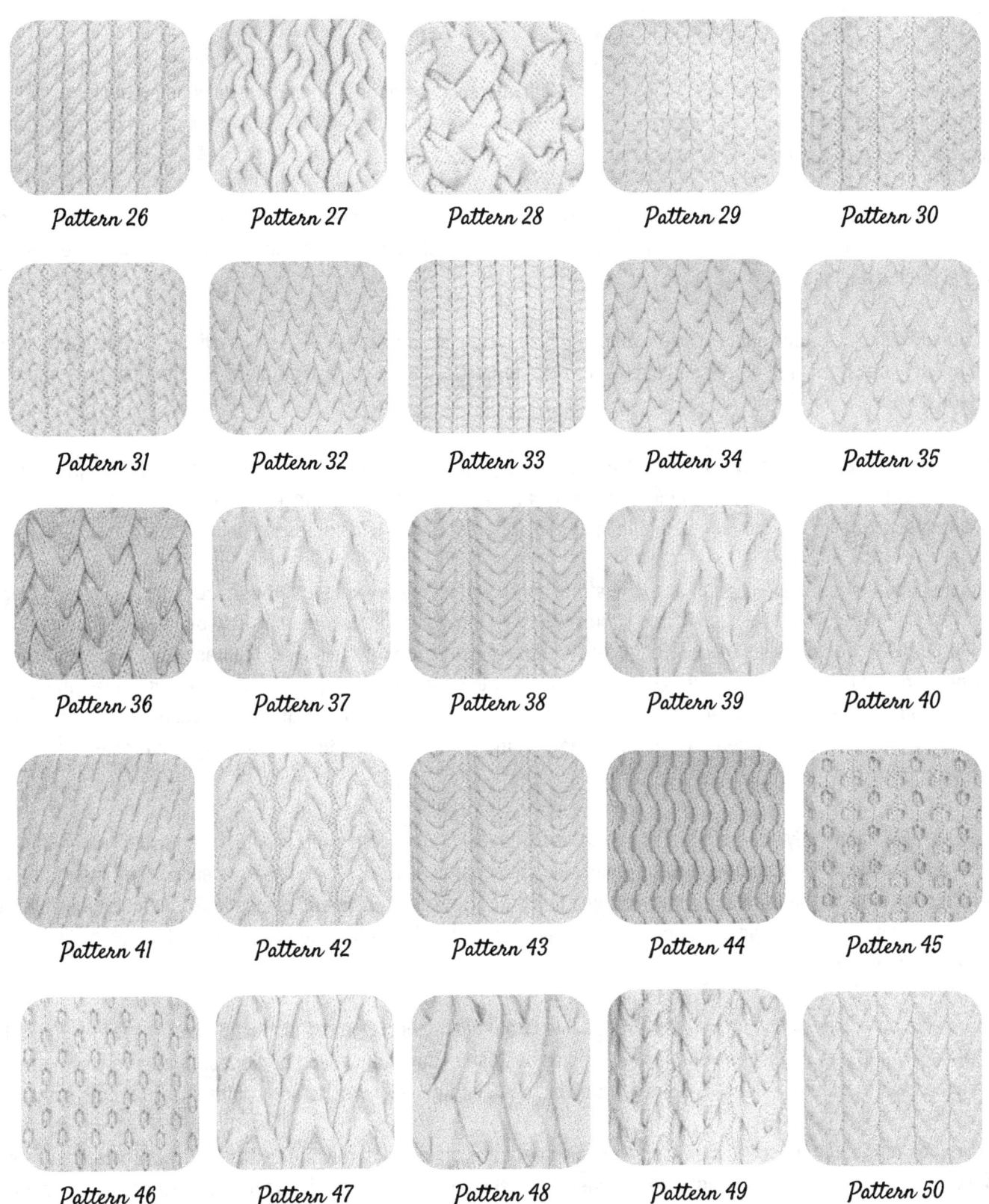

Introduction

The principle of knitting all braids and cables is based on intersected stitches. Their drastically different looks achieve as a result of changing combinations of stitch intersections, which seem endless. Thus appear small and big braids and cables and numerous variations of both.

Different looks and sizes of braids and cables achieve as a result of the intersections different numbers of stitches, to the right or to the left, and working different numbers of vertical rows between the intersected stitches. This is the principle of knitting all braids and cables.

In this book we show various stitch intersections and how insignificant changes in their variations create slightly modified and completely newly looking braids and cables. For this project, we have worked on many different patterns and offer you the best ones.

We also show different sizes of the same and similar-looking large braids and cables, which can be more appropriate for certain sizes of knits, small or big, as some braids and cables look better when they are suitable for a certain size. Large braids can also be used as a center element in knits with different braids and cables.

Most cable-based patterns look tighter and, therefore, better when they are knitted through the back legs, which is the second way of knitting. However, braids and cables with very frequently intersected stitches look better when they are knitted through the front legs, as otherwise the knit fabric comes out too tight. Some cable-based patterns can be knitted both ways, through the front legs or through the back legs, with an insignificant difference in their tightness and quality; whereas others require a specific way of knitting, through the front legs or through the back legs, as otherwise they do not look good or come out distorted. The patterns that we show, we have tried to knit both ways and recommend you the better options.

Purl stitches that commonly separate braids and cables from each other come out uneven, as knit stitches, on the backside due to stitch intersections. The more purl stitches separate braids and cables from each other, the more even the knit stitches look on the backside. However, one purl stitch between braids and cables looks better as a knit stitch on the backside than two or three stitches do. One purl stitch also looks better between frequently intersected stitches and in varieties of different braids and cables.

There are also other ways to separate braids and cables from each other. One of the most popular ways is slipped down stitches, from top to bottom, between braids and cables, instead of commonly used purl ones. There are also many decorative patterns, including openwork ones, that look very good between braids and cables—and on both sides.

The good look of the bottom edge of braids and cables depends on in which row the first intersections of stitches begin. The bottom edge of some patterns looks better when the first intersections begin in the first row, whereas others look better when the first intersections begin in the third row, or higher.

Consider combining different braids and cables in one pattern. They look even more beautiful when they are mixed. In this project, we show many braids and cables that can be combined in different patterns. You can choose the ones you like and create your own knitting patterns. We offer many braids and cables to choose from. Your job is to create and look beautiful.

— Marina Molo

Recommendations

Two Ways of Knitting Stitches

Knitting through the front legs: Knit through the front leg, inserting the right needle through the stitch from left to right, purl as follows: with the working yarn in front of the stitch, insert the right needle through the stitch from back to front and wrap the working yarn counterclockwise around the tip of the right needle, then pull the working yarn with the right needle through the stitch. Note: The purl stitch that is worked this way sets up the knit stitch to be knitted through the front leg. This method of knitting is the most popular and known as conventional.

Knitting through the back legs: Knit through the back leg, inserting the right needle through the stitch from front to back, purl as follows: with the working yarn in front of the stitch, insert the right needle through the stitch from back to front, then move the working yarn under the right needle and pull it with the needle through the stitch. Note: The purl stitch that is worked this way sets up the knit stitch to be knitted through the back leg.

How to Work the Edge Stitches

Unless indicated otherwise, when knit stitch follows yarn over, the working yarn goes from the front of the needle towards the back. In this case, the description reads "yarn over counterclockwise." When purl stitch follows yarn over, the working yarn goes from the behind the needle towards the front. In this case, the description reads "yarn over clockwise."

How to Work Edge Stitches

The first way: Slip the first edge stitch; purl the last edge stitch as if to purl in knitting through back leg as follows: with the working yarn in front of the stitch, insert the right needle through the stitch from back to front, then move the working yarn under the right needle and pull it with the needle through the stitch. Note: Regardless of the method of knitting, through the front legs or through the back legs, purl the last edge stitch as if to purl in knitting through the back leg, as this way of working the last edge stitch creates more tight and even edges.

The second way: Knit both the first edge stitch and the last one through the front legs (or, depending on pattern, through the back legs). Note: This way of working the edge stitches is used in patterns in which otherwise the left edge comes out loose and slightly stretchy. This way of working the edge stitches creates even edges on both sides.

How to Do Yarn Over

Unless indicated otherwise, when knit stitch follows yarn over, the working yarn goes from the front of the needle towards the back. In this case, the description reads "yarn over counterclockwise." When purl stitch follows yarn over, the working yarn goes from the behind the needle towards the front. In this case, the description reads "yarn over clockwise."

How to Bind off Braids and Cables

The first method: After the last row of intersected stitches, turn your work over, to the Back Side; slip all stitches from the left needle to the right one, as a result, the working yarn is at the end of the row; turn your work over, to the Front Side; slip 2 stitches from the left needle to the right one, then insert the left needle through the 1st slipped stitch from left to right and pass it over the 2nd one (now, there is 1 stitch on the right needle), *slip 1 stitch from the left needle to the right one, insert the left needle through the 1st stitch on the right needle from left to right and pass it over the 2nd one (now, there is 1 stitch on the right needle)* repeat from * to * until the end of the row.

Note: This method is appropriate for binding off frequently intersected stitches and patterns that do not require an additional trimming, as this way of binding off creates a tight chain of small stitches that look already finished. For patterns that do require trimming, knit the last row of intersected stitches and bind off loosely, using larger needles than the working ones.

The second method: Slip the edge stitch onto the right needle, knit the next 1, then insert the left needle through the slipped edge stitch from left to right and pass it over the knitted stitch (now, there is 1 stitch on the right needle), *knit the next 1, then insert the left needle through the 1st stitch on the right needle from left to right and pass it over the knitted one (now, there is 1 stitch on the right needle)* repeat from * to * until the end of the row.

How to Count Rows

Count the edge stitches, instead of rows, as counting the actual rows, especially in complicated patterns, can be difficult, or impossible. Each edge stitch is equal to 2 rows. Count the chain of the edge stitches as follows: 2, 4, 6, 8, 10, etc. It's fast and easy.

Pattern 1

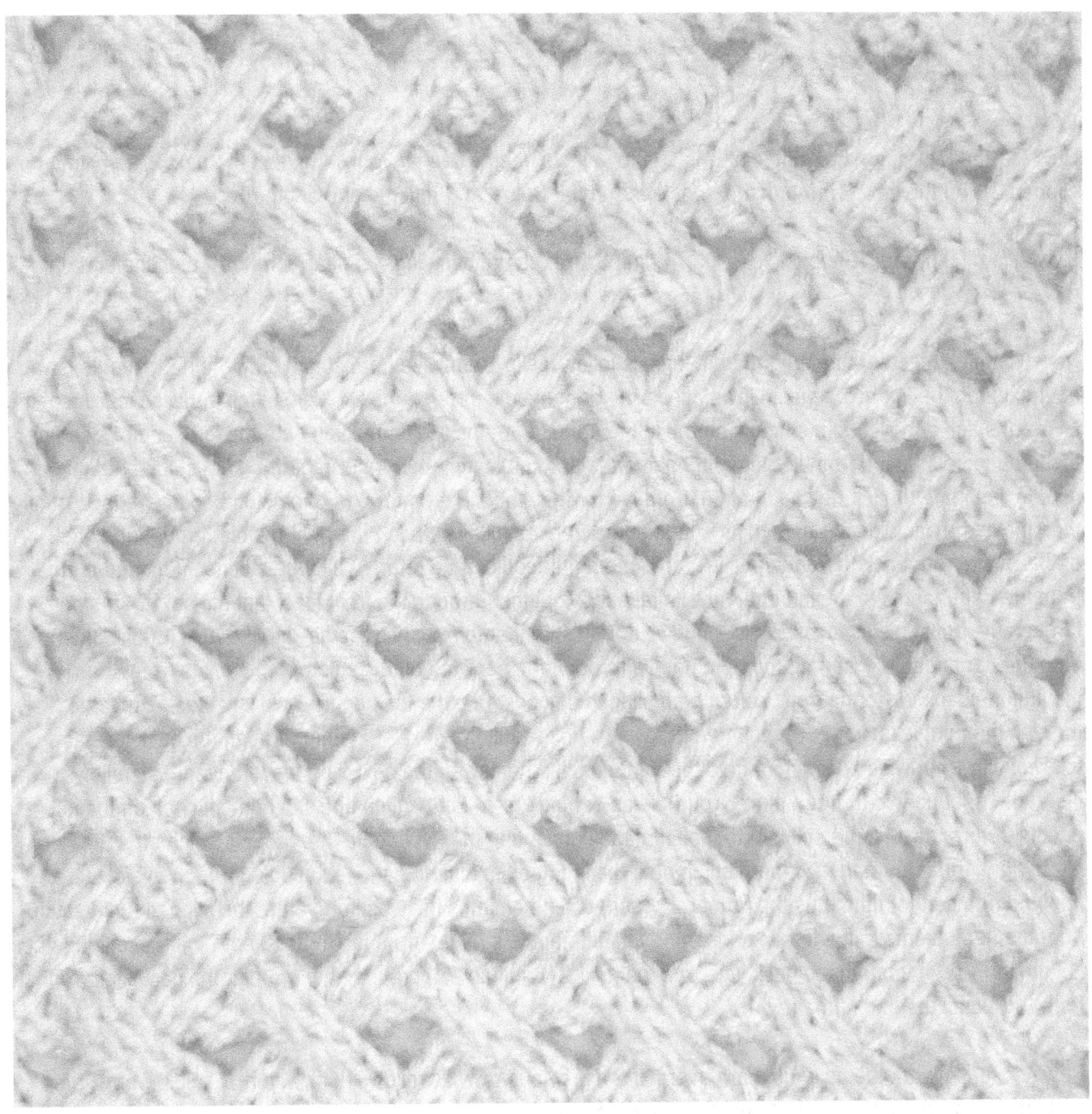

Cast on a multiple of 8, plus 2 edge stitches. Eight-stitch repeat. Repeat rows: 1-8.
Needles: U.S. no. 6 (4 mm). The edge stitches are not included in the description below and must be added. Slip the first edge stitch; purl the last edge stitch.

Knit through the back leg; purl as follows: with the working yarn in front of the stitch, insert the right needle through the stitch from back to front, move the working yarn under the right needle and pull it with the needle through the stitch. The purl stitch that is worked this way sets up the knit stitch to be knitted through the back leg.

Description:

Row 1: *Purl 2 through the front legs, slip 2 onto a cable needle behind your work, knit the next 2, then knit the slipped 2, purl the next 2 through the front legs* repeat from * to * until the end of the row.

Row 2: *Knit 2 through the back legs, purl 4, knit 2 through the back legs* repeat from * to * until the end of the row.

Row 3: *Knit 2 together through the front legs as follows: slip 1 purlwise (purl stitch) onto the right needle; swap the next 2 on the left needle as follows: insert the right needle through the 2nd (knit) stitch purlwise in front of the 1st (purl) stitch and slip both stitches off the left needle, return the 1st (purl) stitch onto the left needle, inserting the left needle straight, from left to right, behind the 2nd (knit) stitch, then return the 2nd (knit) stitch onto the left needle, inserting the left needle straight, from left to right, thus the former 2nd (knit) stitch becomes the 1st stitch, then move the back leg of this 1st (knit) stitch to the front as follows: insert the right needle through the back leg of this stitch from back to front and slip it onto the right needle, then return 2 slipped stitches (knit and purl) from the right needle to the left one, now knit these 2 together through the front legs; knit the next 2 together through the front legs as follows: slip 1 purlwise (purl stitch) onto the right needle, slip the next 1 (knit stitch) onto the right needle, inserting the right needle through the back leg of this stitch from back to front, thus moving the back leg to the front, return both slipped stitches onto the left needle, now knit these 2 together through the front legs; yarn over counterclockwise 4 times; knit the next 2 together through the back legs as follows: slip 1 purlwise (knit stitch) onto the right needle, then swap the next 2 on the left needle as follows: insert the right needle through the 2nd (purl) stitch behind the 1st (knit) stitch and slip both stitches off the left needle, return the 1st (knit) stitch onto the left needle, inserting the left needle through this stitch straight, from left to right, then return the 2nd (purl) stitch onto the left needle, inserting the left needle through this stitch straight, from left to right, thus the former 2nd (purl) stitch becomes the 1st stitch, return the slipped (knit) stitch from the right needle to the left one, inserting the left needle straight, from left to right, now knit these 2 together (1 knit and 1 purl) through the back legs; knit the next 2 (1 knit and 1 purl) together through the back legs* repeat from * to * until the end of the row.

Row 4: *Purl 2, work the next 4 (4 yarn overs of the previous row) as follows: knit 1, purl 1, knit 1, purl 1, then purl the next 2* repeat from * to * until the end of the row.

Row 5: Knit 2 through the back legs, *purl 4 through the front legs, slip 2 onto a cable needle in front of your work, knit the next 2, then knit the slipped 2* repeat from * to * until the end of the row before the edge stitch—

the last 6 stitches—purl 4 through the front legs, knit 2 through the back legs.

Row 6: *Purl 2, knit 4 through the back legs, purl 2* repeat from * to * until the end of the row.

Row 7: *Yarn over counterclockwise 2 times, knit 2 together through the back legs as follows: slip 1 purlwise (knit stitch) onto the right needle, swap the next 2 on the left needle as follows: insert the right needle through the 2nd (purl) stitch purlwise behind the 1st (knit) stitch and slip both stitches off the left needle, return the 1st (knit) stitch onto the left needle, inserting the left needle straight, from left to right, then return the 2nd (purl) stitch onto the left needle, straight, inserting the left needle from left to right, thus the former 2nd stitch (purl) becomes the 1st stitch, return the slipped (knit) stitch from the right needle to the left one, inserting the left needle straight, from left to right, now, knit these 2 together through the back legs; knit the next 2 together through the back legs; knit the next 2 together through the front legs as follows: slip 1 (purl stitch) purlwise onto the right needle, swap the next 2 on the left needle as follows: insert the right needle purlwise through the 2nd (knit) stitch in front of the 1st (purl) stitch and slip both stitches off the left needle, return the 1st (purl) stitch onto the left needle, inserting the left needle straight, from left to right, then return the 2nd (knit) stitch onto the left needle, inserting the left needle straight, from left to right, thus the former 2nd (knit) stitch becomes the 1st stitch, then slip this 1st (knit) stitch onto the right needle, inserting the right needle through the back leg from back to front, thus moving the back leg of this stitch to the front, then return both slipped stitches (knit and purl) from the right needle to the left one, now, knit these 2 together through the front legs; knit the next 2 together through the front legs as follows: slip 1 purlwise (purl stitch) onto the right needle, slip the next 1 (knit stitch) onto the right needle, inserting the right needle through the back leg from back to front, thus moving the back leg to the front, return both slipped stitches from the right needle to the left needle, now, knit these 2 together through the front legs; then yarn over counterclockwise 2 times* repeat from * to * until the end of the row.

Row 8: *Knit 1 (yarn over of the previous row), purl 1 (yarn over of the previous row), purl 4, knit 1 (yarn over of the previous row), purl 1 (yarn over of the previous row)* repeat from * to * until the end of the row.

Repeat rows: 1-8.

Bind off as follows: After the last row 2, turn your work over; the Front Side: slip all the stitches from the left needle to the right one, as a result, the working yarn is at the end of the row; turn your work over; the Back Side: slip 2 stitches from the left needle to the right one, insert the left needle through the 1st slipped stitch from left to right and pass it over the 2nd stitch (now, there is 1 stitch on the right needle), *slip 1 from the left needle to the right one, insert the left needle through the 1st stitch on the right needle from left to right and pass it over the 2nd stitch (now, there is 1 stitch on the right needle)* repeat from * to * until the end of the row.

Note: For trimming, bind off loosely using larger needles than the working ones, in order to create a larger chain of edge stitches, as this type of binding off creates a tight chain of small edge stitches that look already finished.

Pattern 2

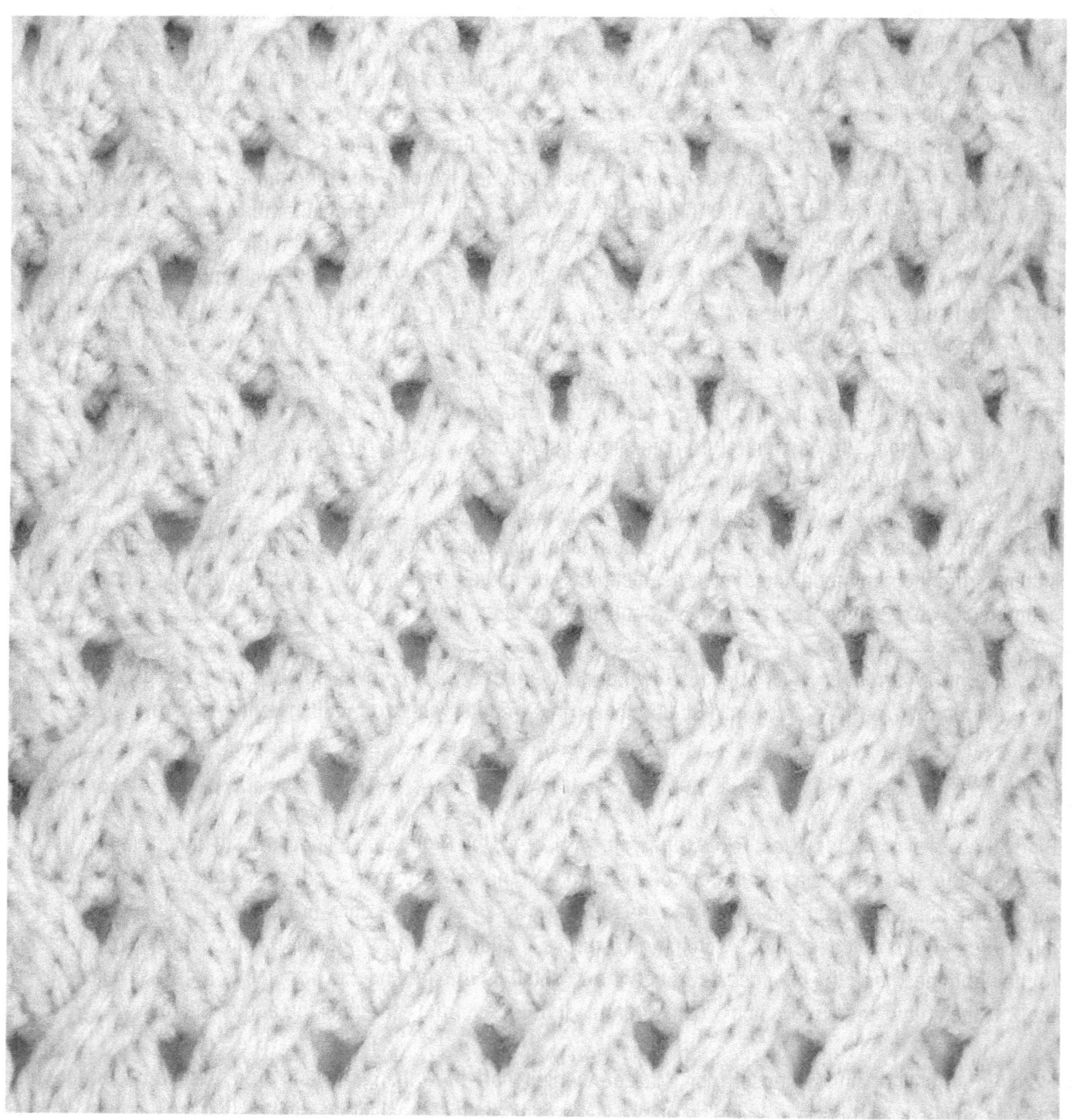

Cast on a multiple of 6, plus 2 edge stitches. Six-stitch repeat. Repeat rows: 1-8. The edge stitches are not included in the description below and must be added. Slip the first edge stitch; purl the last edge stitch as if to purl in knitting through the back leg as follows: insert the right needle through the stitch from back to front, move the working yarn under the right needle and pull it with the needle through the stitch.

Knit through the front leg; purl as follows: with the working yarn in front of the stitch, wrap the working yarn counterclockwise around the tip of the right needle, then pull the working yarn with the needle through the stitch. The purl stitch that is worked this way sets up the knit stitch to be knitted through the front leg.

Description:

Row 1: *Purl 1 through the front leg, slip 2 onto a cable needle in front of your work, knit the next 2, then knit the slipped 2, purl 1* repeat from * to * until the end of the row.

Row 2: *Knit 1, purl 4, knit 1* repeat from * to * until the end of the row.

Row 3: *Knit 2 together, knit 1, yarn over counterclockwise 2 times, knit 1, knit the next 2 together through the back legs as follows: slip 1 knitwise (knit stitch) onto the right needle, slip the next 1 knitwise (purl stitch) onto the right needle, return both slipped stitches from the right needle to the left one, now knit 2 together through the back legs* repeat from * to * until the end of the row.

Row 4: *Purl 2, purl 1 (yarn over of the previous row) as if to purl in knitting through the back leg as follows: insert the right needle through the stitch from back to front, move the working yarn under the right needle and pull it with the needle through the stitch, knit 1 (yarn over of the previous row), purl 2* repeat from * to * until the end of the row.

Row 5: Knit 2, *purl 2 (note: purl the 2nd (knit) stitch through the front leg), slip 2 onto a cable needle behind your work, knit the next 2, then knit the slipped 2* repeat from * to * until the end of the row before the edge stitch—the last 4 stitches—purl 2 (note: purl the 2nd (knit) stitch through the front leg), knit 2.

Row 6: *Purl 2, knit 2, purl 2* repeat from * to * until the end of the row.

Row 7: Yarn over counterclockwise, *knit 1, knit 2 together through the back legs as follows: slip 1 knitwise (knit stitch) onto the right needle, slip the next 1 knitwise (purl stitch) onto the right needle, return both slipped stitches from the right needle to the left one, now knit 2 together through the back legs, then knit the next 2 together, knit 1, yarn over counterclockwise 2 times* repeat from * to * until the end of the row before the edge stitch—the last 6 stitches— knit 1, knit 2 together through the back legs as follows: slip 1 knitwise (knit stitch) onto the right needle, slip the next 1 knitwise (purl stitch), return both slipped stitches from the right needle to the left one, now knit 2 together through the back legs, then knit 2 together, knit 1, yarn over counterclockwise.

Row 8: Knit 1 (yarn over of the previous row), *purl 4, purl 1 (yarn over of the previous row) as if to purl in knitting through the back leg as follows: insert the right needle through the stitch from back to front, move the working yarn under the right needle and pull it with the needle through the stitch, knit 1 (yarn over of the previous row)* repeat from * to * until the end of the row before the edge stitch—the last 5 stitches—purl 4, knit 1 (yarn over of the previous row).

Repeat rows: 1-8.

Bind off as follows: After the last row 1, turn your work over; the Back Side: slip all the stitches from the left needle to the right one, as a result, the working yarn is at the end of the row; turn your work over; the Front Side: slip 2 stitches from the left needle to the right one, insert the left needle through the 1st slipped stitch from left to right and pass it over the 2nd stitch (now, there is 1 stitch on the right needle), *slip 1 from the left needle to the right one, insert the left needle through the 1st stitch on the right needle from left to right and pass it over the 2nd stitch (now, there is 1 stitch on the right needle)* repeat from * to * until the end of the row.

Note: For trimming, bind off loosely using larger needles than the working ones, in order to create a larger chain of edge stitches, as this type of binding off creates a tight chain of small edge stitches that look already finished.

Pattern 3

Cast on a multiple of 6, plus 3, and plus 2 edge stitches. Six-stitch repeat. Repeat rows: 1-8. The edge stitches are not included in the description below and must be added. Slip the first edge stitch; purl the last edge stitch.

Knit through the back leg; purl as follows: with the working yarn in front of your work, insert the right needle through the stitch from back to front, move the working yarn under the right needle and pull it with the needle through the stitch. The purl stitch that is worked this way sets up the knit stitch to be knitted through the back leg.

Description:

Row 1: *Slip 3 onto a cable needle in front of your work, knit the next 3, knit the slipped 3* repeat from * to * until the end of the row before the edge stitch, knit 3.

Row 2: Purl all the stitches.

Row 3: Knit all the stitches.

Row 4: Purl all the stitches.

Row 5: Knit 3, *slip 3 onto a cable needle behind your work, knit the next 3, knit the slipped 3* repeat from * to * until the end of the row.

Row 6: Purl all the stitches.

Row 7: Knit all the stitches.

Row 8: Purl all the stitches.

Repeat rows: 1-8.

Bind off as follows: After the last row 1, turn your work over; the Back Side: slip all the stitches from the left needle to the right one, as a result, the working yarn is at the end of the row; turn your work over; the Front Side: slip 2 stitches from the left needle to the right one, insert the left needle through the 1st slipped stitch from left to right and pass it over the 2nd stitch (now, there is 1 stitch on the right needle), *slip 1 from the left needle to the right one, insert the left needle through the 1st stitch on the right needle from left to right and pass it over the 2nd stitch (now, there is 1 stitch on the right needle)* repeat from * to * until the end of the row.

Note: For trimming, bind off loosely using larger needles than the working ones, in order to create a larger chain of edge stitches, as this type of binding off creates a tight chain of small edge stitches that look already finished.

Pattern 4

Cast on a multiple of 8, plus 4, and plus 2 edge stitches. Eight-stitch repeat. Repeat rows: 1-8. The edge stitches are not included in the description below and must be added. Slip the first edge stitch; purl the last edge stitch.

Knit through the back leg; purl as follows: with the working yarn in front of the work, insert the right needle through the stitch from back to front, move the working yarn under the right needle and pull it with the needle through the stitch. The purl stitch that is worked this way sets up the knit stitch to be knitted through the back leg.

Description:

Row 1: *Slip 4 onto a cable needle in front of your work, knit the next 4, knit the slipped 4* repeat from * to * until the end of the row before the edge stitch, knit 4.

Row 2: Purl all the stitches.

Row 3: Knit all the stitches.

Row 4: Purl all the stitches.

Row 5: Knit 4, *slip 4 onto a cable needle behind your work, knit the next 4, knit the slipped 4* repeat from * to * until the end of the row.

Row 6: Purl all the stitches.

Row 7: Knit all the stitches.

Row 8: Purl all the stitches.

Repeat rows: 1-8.

Bind off as follows: After the last row 1, turn your work over; the Back Side: slip all the stitches from the left needle to the right one, as a result, the working yarn is at the end of the row; turn your work over; the Front Side: slip 2 stitches from the left needle to the right one, insert the left needle through the 1st slipped stitch from left to right and pass it over the 2nd stitch (now, there is 1 stitch on the right needle), *slip 1 from the left needle to the right one, insert the left needle through the 1st stitch on the right needle from left to right and pass it over the 2nd stitch (now, there is 1 stitch on the right needle)* repeat from * to * until the end of the row.

Note: For trimming, bind off loosely using larger needles than the working ones, in order to create a larger chain of edge stitches, as this type of binding off creates a tight chain of small edge stitches that look already finished.

Pattern 5

Cast on a multiple of 9, plus 2 edge stitches. Nine-stitch repeat. Repeat rows: 1-4. The edge stitches are not included in the description and must be added. Slip the first edge stitch; purl the last stitch.

Knit through the back leg; purl as follows: with the working yarn in front of the work, insert the right needle through the stitch from back to front, move the working yarn under the right needle and pull it with the needle through the stitch. The purl stitch that is worked this way sets up the knit stitch to be knitted through the back leg.

Description:

Row 1: *Slip 3 onto a cable needle in front of your work, knit the next 3, then knit the slipped 3, knit the next 3* repeat from * to * until the end of the row.

Row 2: Purl all the stitches.

Row 3: *Knit 3, slip the next 3 onto a cable needle behind your work, knit the next 3, then knit the slipped 3* repeat from * to * until the end of the row.

Row 4: Purl all the stitches.

Repeat rows: 1-4.

Bind off as follows: After the last row 1, turn your work over; the Back Side: slip all the stitches from the left needle to the right one, as a result, the working yarn is at the end of the row; turn your work over; the Front Side: slip 2 stitches from the left needle to the right one, insert the left needle through the 1st slipped stitch from left to right and pass it over the 2nd stitch (now, there is 1 stitch on the right needle), *slip 1 from the left needle to the right one, insert the left needle through the 1st stitch on the right needle from left to right and pass it over the 2nd stitch (now, there is 1 stitch on the right needle)* repeat from * to * until the end of the row.

Note: For trimming, bind off loosely using larger needles than the working ones, in order to create a larger chain of edge stitches, as this type of binding off creates a tight chain of small edge stitches that look already finished.

Pattern 6

Cast on a multiple of 18, plus 2, plus 2 edge stitches. Eighteen-stitch repeat. Repeat rows: 1-12. The edge stitches are not included in the description below and must be added. Slip the first edge stitch; purl the last edge stitch.

Knit through the back leg; purl as follows: with the working yarn in front of the stitch, insert the right needle through the stitch from back to front, move the working yarn under the right needle and pull it with the needle through the stitch. The purl stitch that is worked this way sets up the knit stitch to be knitted through the back leg.

Description:

Row 1: *Purl 2, slip 4 onto a cable needle in front of your work, knit the next 4, then knit the slipped 4, knit 8* repeat from * to * until the end of the row before the edge stitch, purl 2.

Row 2: *Knit 2, purl 16* repeat from * to * until the end of the row before the edge stitch, knit 2.

Row 3: *Purl 2, knit 16* repeat from * to * until the end of the row before the edge stitch, purl 2.

Row 4: *Knit 2, purl 16* repeat from * to * until the end of the row before the edge stitch, knit 2.

Row 5: *Purl 2, knit 16 * repeat from * to * until the end of the row before the edge stitch, purl 2.

Row 6: *Knit 2, purl 16* repeat from * to * until the end of the row before the edge stitch, knit 2.

Row 7: *Purl 2, knit 8, slip 4 onto a cable needle behind your work, knit the next 4, then knit the slipped 4* repeat from * to * until the end of the row before the edge stitch, purl 2.

Row 8: *Knit 2, purl 16* repeat from * to * until the end of the row before the edge stitch, knit 2.

Row 9: *Purl 2, knit 16* repeat from * to * until the end of the row before the edge stitch, purl 2.

Row 10: *Knit 2, purl 16 * repeat from * to * until the end of the row before the edge stitch, knit 2.

Row 11: *Purl 2, knit 16* repeat from * to * until the end of the row before the edge stitch, purl 2.

Row 12: *Knit 2, purl 16* repeat from * to * until the end of the row before the edge stitch, knit 2.

Repeat rows: 1-12.

Bind off as follows: After the last row 1, turn your work over; the Back Side: slip all the stitches from the left needle to the right one, as a result, the working yarn is at the end of the row; turn your work over; the Front Side: slip 2 stitches from the left needle to the right one, insert the left needle through the 1st slipped stitch from left to right and pass it over the 2nd stitch (now, there is 1 stitch on the right needle), *slip 1 from the left needle to the right one, insert the left needle through the 1st stitch on the right needle from left to right and pass it over the 2nd stitch (now, there is 1 stitch on the right needle)* repeat from * to * until the end of the row.

Note: For trimming, bind off loosely using larger needles than the working ones, in order to create a larger chain of edge stitches, as this type of binding off creates a tight chain of small edge stitches that look already finished.

Pattern 7

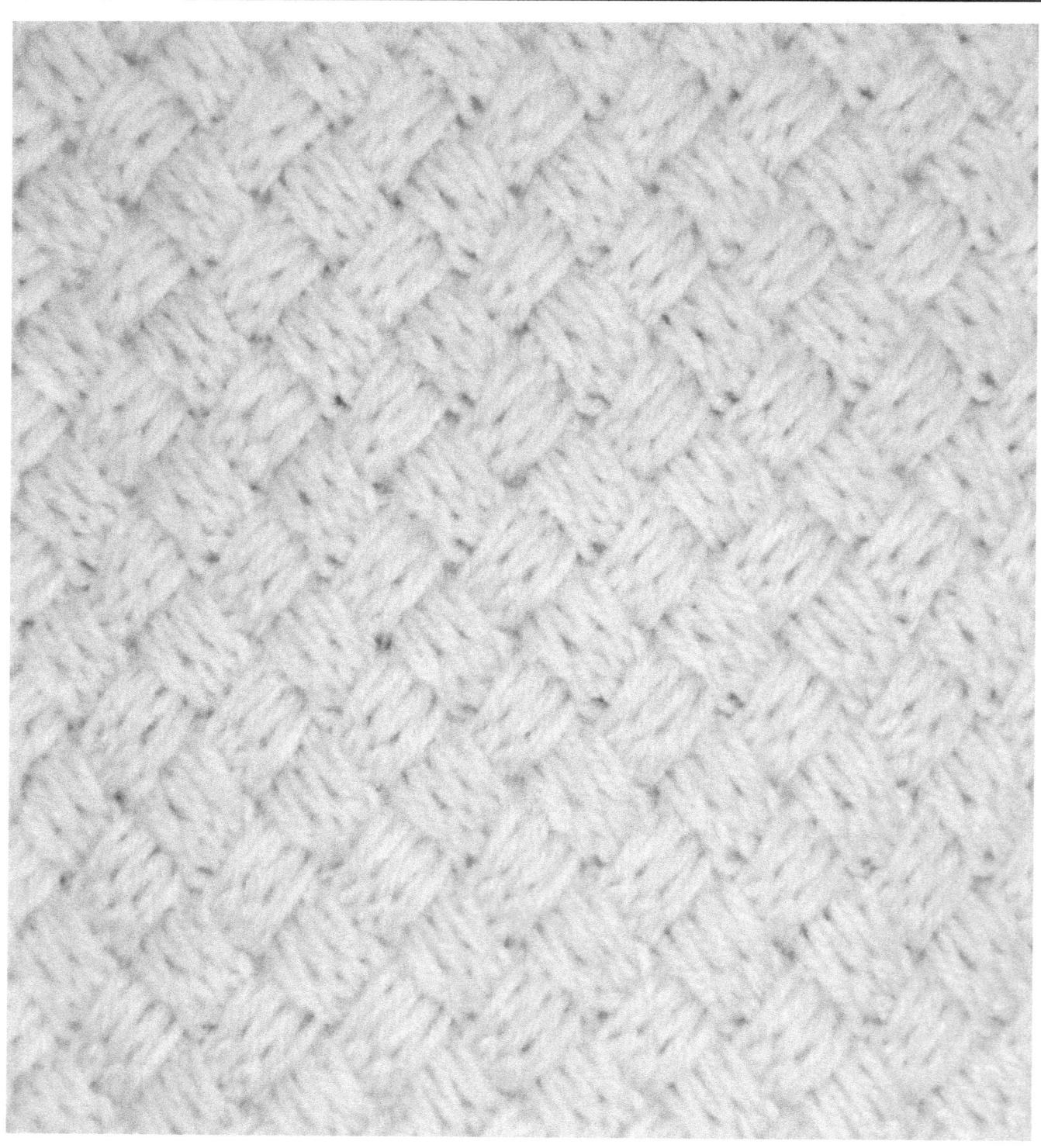

Cast on a multiple of 6, plus 2 edge stitches. Six-stitch repeat. Repeat rows: 1-4. Needles: U.S. no. 6 (4 mm).

Knit through the back leg, purl as follows: with the working yarn in front of the stitch, insert the right needle through the stitch from back to front, move the working yarn under the right needle, then pull it with the needle through the stitch. The purl stitch that is worked this way sets up the knit stitch to be knitted through the back leg.

Description:

Row 1 (Back Side): Purl the edge stitch, *yarn over counterclockwise, purl 1* repeat from * to * until the end of the row, purl the edge stitch.

Row 2 (Front Side): Slip the edge stitch, slip each knit stitch purlwise from the left needle to the right one and slip each yarn over off the left needle, leaving it as is, thus creating and moving elongated knit stitches onto the right needle, leave the last edge stitch on the left needle (now, the working yarn is at the end of the right needle); *intersect 6 stitches to the right as follows: counting from left to right, insert the left needle through the 4th, 5th, and 6th stitches purlwise behind your work and slip all 6 stitches off the right needle, then pick up the 1st, 2nd, and 3rd stitches onto the right needle purlwise and slip them onto the left needle, thus these 6 stitches are intersected to the right on the left needle* repeat from * to * until the end of the row, thus moving all the stitches from the right needle to the left one. Now, knit the first edge stitch, knit all the stitches, knit the last edge stitch.

Row 3 (Back Side): Purl the first edge stitch, *yarn over counterclockwise, purl 1* repeat from * to * until the end of the row, purl the last edge stitch.

Row 4 (Front Side): Slip the edge stitch onto the right needle, slip each knit stitch from the left needle to the right one and slip each yarn over off the left needle, leaving it as is, thus creating and moving elongated knit stitches onto the right needle; leave the last edge stitch on the left needle (now, the working yarn is at the end of the right needle); slip the first 3 stitches from the right needle to the left one, *intersect the next 6 stitches to the left as follows: counting from left to right, insert the left needle through the 4th, 5th, and 6th stitches in front of your work and slip all 6 stitches off the right needle, then pick up the first 3 stitches onto the right needle purlwise behind your work and slip them onto the left needle; now these 6 stitches are intersected to the left* repeat from * to * until the end of the row, slip the last 3 stitches and the edge stitch from the right needle to the left needle. Now, knit the first edge stitch, knit all the stitches, knit the last edge stitch.

Repeat rows: 1-4.

Bind off as follows: After the last row 4, turn your work over; the Back Side: slip all the stitches from the left needle to the right one, as a result, the working yarn is at the end of the right needle, then turn your work over; the Front Side: slip 2 purlwise from the left needle to the right one, insert the left needle through the front leg of the 1st slipped stitch from left to right and pass it over the 2nd stitch (now, there is 1 stitch on the right needle), *slip 1 purlwise from the left needle to the right one, insert the left needle through the front leg of the 1st stitch on the right needle from left to right and pass it over the 2nd stitch (now, there is 1 stitch on the right needle)* repeat from * to * until the end of the row.

Note: For trimming, bind off loosely using larger needles than the working ones, in order to create a larger chain of edge stitches, as this type of binding off creates a tight chain of small edge stitches that look already finished.

Pattern 8

Cast on 30 stitches for the braid, plus 4 adjacent stitches (2 at each side of the braid). The number of adjacent stitches is optional. Repeat rows: 1-8.

Knit through the back leg; purl as follows: with the working yarn in front of the stitch, insert the right needle through the stitch from back to front, move the working yarn under the right needle and pull it with the needle through the stitch. The purl stitch that is worked this way sets up the knit stitch to be knitted through the back leg.

Description:

Row 1: Purl 2, knit 30, purl 2.

Row 2: Knit 2, purl 30, knit 2.

Row 3: Purl 2, slip 5 onto a cable needle in front of your work, knit the next 5, knit the slipped 5, knit 10, slip the next 5 onto a cable needle behind your work, knit the next 5, knit the slipped 5, purl 2.

Row 4: Knit 2, purl 30, knit 2.

Row 5: Purl 2, knit 30, purl 2.

Row 6: Knit 2, purl 30, knit 2.

Row 7: Purl 2, knit 5, slip the next 5 onto a cable needle behind your work, knit the next 5, knit the slipped 5, slip the next 5 onto a cable needle in front of your work, knit the next 5, knit the slipped 5, knit 5, purl 2.

Row 8: Knit 2, purl 30, knit 2.

Repeat rows: 1-8.

Bind off as follows: After the last row 3, turn your work over; the Back Side: slip all the stitches from the left needle to the right one, as a result, the working yarn is at the end of the right needle, then turn your work over; the Front Side: slip 2 purlwise from the left needle to the right one, insert the left needle through the front leg of the 1st slipped stitch from left to right and pass it over the 2nd stitch (now, there is 1 stitch on the right needle); *slip 1 purlwise from the left needle to the right one, insert the left needle through the front leg of the 1st stitch on the right needle from left to right and pass it over the 2nd stitch (now, there is 1 stitch on the right needle)* repeat from * to * until the end of the row.

Note: For trimming, bind off loosely using larger needles than the working ones, in order to create a larger chain of edge stitches, as this type of binding off creates a tight chain of small edge stitches that look already finished.

Pattern 9

Cast on 32 stitches for the braid, plus 4 adjacent stitches (2 at each side of the braid). The number of adjacent stitches is optional. Repeat rows: 1-10.

Knit through the back leg; purl as follows: with the working yarn in front of the stitch, insert the right needle through the stitch from back to front, move the working yarn under the right needle and pull it with the needle through the stitch. The purl stitch that is worked this way sets up the knit stitch to be knitted through the back leg.

Description:

Row 1: Purl 2, knit 32, purl 2.

Row 2: Knit 2, purl 32, knit 2.

Row 3: Purl 2, slip 8 onto a cable needle behind your work, knit the next 8, knit the slipped 8, slip 8 onto a cable needle in front of your work, knit the next 8, knit the slipped 8, purl 2.

Row 4: Knit 2, purl 32, knit 2.

Row 5: Purl 2, knit 32, purl 2.

Row 6: Knit 2, purl 32, knit 2.

Row 7: Purl 2, knit 32, purl 2.

Row 8: Knit 2, purl 32, knit 2.

Row 9: Purl 2, knit 32, purl 2.

Row 10: Knit 2, purl 32, knit 2.

Repeat rows: 1-10.

Bind off as follows: After the last row 3, turn your work over; the Back Side: slip all the stitches from the left needle to the right one, as a result, the working yarn is at the end of the right needle, then turn your work over; the Front Side: slip 2 purlwise from the left needle to the right one, insert the left needle through the front leg of the 1st slipped stitch from left to right and pass it over the 2nd stitch (now, there is 1 stitch on the right needle), *slip 1 purlwise from the left needle to the right one, insert the left needle through the front leg of the 1st stitch on the right needle from left to right and pass it over the 2nd stitch (now, there is 1 stitch on the right needle)* repeat from * to * until the end of the row. Note: For trimming, bind off loosely using larger needles than the working ones, in order to create a larger chain of edge stitches, as this type of binding off creates a tight chain of small edge stitches that look already finished.

Pattern 10

Cast on 24 stitches for the braid, plus 4 adjacent stitches (2 at each side of the braid). The number of adjacent stitches is optional. Repeat rows: 1-8. Knit tightly.

Knit through the back leg; purl as follows: with the working yarn in front of the stitch, insert the right needle through the stitch from back to front, move the working yarn under the right needle and pull it with the needle through the stitch. The purl stitch that is worked this way sets up the knit stitch to be knitted through the back leg.

Description:

Row 1: Purl 2, knit 24, purl 2.

Row 2: Knit 2, purl 24, knit 2.

Row 3: Purl 2, slip 6 onto a cable needle behind your work, knit the next 6, then knit the slipped 6, slip the next 6 onto a cable needle in front of your work, knit the next 6, then knit the slipped 6, purl 2.

Row 4: Knit 2, purl 24, knit 2.

Row 5: Purl 2, knit 24, purl 2.

Row 6: Knit 2, purl 24, knit 2.

Row 7: Purl 2, knit 24, purl 2.

Row 8: Knit 2, purl 24, knit 2.

Repeat rows: 1-8.

Bind off as follows: After the last row 3, turn your work over; the Back Side: slip all the stitches from the left needle to the right one, as a result, the working yarn is at the end of the right needle, then turn your work over; the Front Side: slip 2 purlwise from the left needle to the right one, insert the left needle through the front leg of the 1st slipped stitch from left to right and pass it over the 2nd stitch (now, there is 1 stitch on the right needle), *slip 1 purlwise from the left needle to the right one, insert the left needle through the front leg of the 1st stitch on the right needle from left to right and pass it over the 2nd stitch (now, there is 1 stitch on the right needle)* repeat from * to * until the end of the row.

Note: For trimming, bind off loosely using larger needles than the working ones, in order to create a larger chain of edge stitches, as this type of binding off creates a tight chain of small edge stitches that look already finished.

Pattern 11

Cast on 30 stitches for the braid, plus 4 adjacent stitches (2 at each side of the braid). The number of adjacent stitches is optional. Repeat rows: 1-8.

Knit through the back leg; purl as follows: with the working yarn in front of the stitch, insert the right needle through the stitch from back to front, move the working yarn under the right needle and pull it with the needle through the stitch. The purl stitch that is worked this way sets up the knit stitch to be knitted through the back leg.

Description:

Row 1: Purl 2, knit 30, purl 2.

Row 2: Knit 2, purl 30, knit 2.

Row 3: Purl 2, knit only 20, then, leaving the rest of the stitches on the left needle, turn your work over; the Back Side: slip 1, purl the next 9, then, leaving the rest of the stitches on the left needle, turn your work over; the Front Side: slip 1, knit 9, then turn your work over; the Back Side: slip 1, purl 9, then turn your work over; the Front Side: Take a cable needle. Slip 1 from the left needle onto the cable needle, knit 9 using the cable needle, thus moving 10 center stitches from the left needle onto the cable needle. Keep the working yarn and the cable needle with 10 center stitches in front of your work. Slip 10 stitches from the right needle to the left one, inserting the left needle from back to front, thus moving the front legs to the back. Slip 10 center stitches purlwise from the cable needle to the right needle. Now, work the stitches on the left needle as follows: knit 20, purl 2.

Row 4: Knit 2, purl 30, knit 2.

Row 5: Purl 2, knit 30, purl 2.

Row 6: Knit 2, purl 30, knit 2.

Row 7: Purl 2, knit only 20, then, leaving the rest of the stitches on the left needle, turn your work over; the Back Side: slip 1, purl 9, then, leaving the rest of the stitches on the left needle, turn your work over; the Front Side: slip 1, knit 9, then turn your work over; the Back Side: slip 1, purl 9, then turn your work over; the Front Side: Take a cable needle. Slip 1 from the left needle to the cable needle, knit the next 9 using the cable needle, thus moving 10 center stitches from the left needle to the cable one. Keep the working yarn and the cable needle with 10 center stitches in front of your work. Slip 10 from the left needle to the right one, inserting the right needle through the back legs from back to front, thus moving the back legs to the front. Then slip 10 center stitches purlwise from the cable needle to the right needle. Now, all 30 stitches of the braid are on the right needle, purl the last 2.

Row 8: Knit 2, purl 30, knit 2.

Repeat rows: 1-8.

Bind off as follows: After the last row 3, turn your work over; the Back Side: slip all the stitches from the left needle to the right one, as a result, the working yarn is at the end of the right needle, then turn your work over; the Front Side: slip 2 purlwise from the left needle to the right one, insert the left needle through the front leg of the 1st slipped stitch from left to right and pass it over the 2nd stitch (now, there is 1 stitch on the right needle), *slip 1 purlwise from the left needle to the right one, insert the left needle through the front leg of the 1st stitch on the right needle from left to right and pass it over the 2nd stitch (now, there is 1 stitch on the right needle)* repeat from * to * until the end of the row.

Note: For trimming, bind off loosely using larger needles than the working ones, in order to create a larger chain of edge stitches, as this type of binding off creates a tight chain of small edge stitches that look already finished.

Pattern 12

Cast on a multiple of 10, plus 2 for symmetry, and plus 2 edge stitches. Ten-stitch repeat. Repeat rows: 1-4. The edge stitches are not included in the description below and must be added. Slip the first edge stitch; purl the last edge stitch.

Knit through the back leg; purl as follows: with the working yarn in front of the stitch, insert the right needle through the stitch from back to front, move the working yarn under the right needle and pull it with the needle through the stitch. The purl stitch that is worked this way sets up the knit stitch to be knitted through the back leg.

Description:

Row 1: *Purl 2, slip 4 onto a cable needle behind your work, knit the next 4, then, leaving the rest of the stitches on the left needle, turn your work over; the Back Side: slip 1 onto the right needle, purl 3, then turn your work over; the Front Side: slip 1 onto the right needle, knit 2 through the back legs, knit 1 through the front leg; now knit the slipped 4, which are on the cable needle* repeat from * to * until the end of the row before the edge stitch, purl 2.

Row 2: *Knit 2, purl 8* repeat from * to * until the end of the row before the edge stitch, knit 2.

Row 3: *Purl 2, knit 8 * repeat from * to * until the end of the row before the edge stitch, purl 2.

Row 4: *Knit 2, purl 8 * repeat from * to * until the end of the row before the edge stitch, knit 2.

Repeat rows: 1-4.

Bind off as follows: After the last row 1, turn your work over; the Back Side: slip all the stitches from the left needle to the right one, as a result, the working yarn is at the end of the row; turn your work over; the Front Side: slip 2 stitches from the left needle to the right one, insert the left needle through the 1st slipped stitch from left to right and pass it over the 2nd one (now, there is 1 stitch on the right needle), *slip 1 from the left needle to the right one, now there are 2 stitches on the right needle, insert the left needle from left to right through the 1st stitch on the right needle and pass it over the 2nd one (now, there is 1 stitch on the right needle)* repeat from * to * until the end of the row.

Note: For trimming, bind off loosely using larger needles than the working ones, in order to create a larger chain of edge stitches, as this type of binding off creates a tight chain of small edge stitches that look already finished.

Pattern 13

Cast on 18 stitches for the braid, plus 4 adjacent stitches (2 at each side of the braid). The number of adjacent stitches is optional. Repeat rows: 1-8.

Knit through the back leg; purl as follows: with the working yarn in front of the stitch, insert the right needle through the stitch from back to front, move the working yarn under the right needle and pull it with the needle through the stitch. The purl stitch that is worked this way sets up the knit stitch to be knitted through the back leg.

Description:

Row 1: Purl 2, knit 18, purl 2.

Row 2: Knit 2, purl 18, knit 2.

Row 3: Purl 2, knit only 12, then, leaving the rest of the stitches on the left needle, turn your work over; the Back Side: Slip 1 from the left needle to the right one, purl the next 5, then, leaving the rest of the stitches on the left needle, turn your work over; the Front Side: Take a cable needle. Slip 1 from the left needle to the cable needle, knit the next 5 using the cable needle, thus moving 6 center stitches from the left needle to the cable one. Keep the working yarn and the cable needle with 6 center stitches in front of your work. Slip 6 stitches from the right needle to the left one, inserting the left needle from back to front, thus moving the front legs to the back. Slip 6 center stitches purlwise from the cable needle to the right needle. Now, work the stitches on the left needle as follows: knit 12, purl 2.

Row 4: Knit 2, purl 18, knit 2.

Row 5: Purl 2, knit 18, purl 2.

Row 6: Knit 2, purl 18, knit 2.

Row 7: Purl 2, knit only 12, then, leaving the rest of the stitches on the left needle, turn your work over; the Back side: slip 1 from the left needle to the right one, purl 5, then, leaving the rest of the stitches on the left needle, turn your work over; the Front Side: Take a cable needle. Slip 1 from the left needle to the cable needle, knit the next 5 using the cable needle, thus moving 6 center stitches from the left needle onto the cable one. Keep the working yarn and the cable needle with 6 center stitches in the front of your work. Slip 6 stitches from the left needle to the right one, inserting the right needle through the back legs from back to front, thus moving the back legs to the front. Slip 6 center stitches purlwise from the cable needle to the right one. Now, all 18 stitches of the braid are on the right needle, purl the last 2.

Row 8: Knit 2, purl 18, knit 2.

Repeat rows: 1-8.

Bind off as follows: After the last row 7, turn your work over; the Back Side: slip all the stitches from the left needle to the right one, as a result, the working yarn is at the end of the row; turn your work over; the Front

Side: slip 2 stitches from the left needle to the right one, insert the left needle through the 1st slipped stitch from left to right and pass it over the 2nd one (now, there is 1 stitch on the right needle), *slip 1 from the left needle to the right one (now, there are 2 stitches on the right needle), insert the left needle from left to right through the 1st stitch on the right needle and pass it over the 2nd one (now, there is 1 stitch on the right needle)* repeat from * to * until the end of the row.

Note: For trimming, bind off loosely using larger needles than the working ones, in order to create a larger chain of edge stitches, as this type of binding off creates a tight chain of small edge stitches that look already finished.

Pattern 14

Cast on 24 stitches for the braid, plus 4 adjacent stitches (2 at each side of the braid). The number of adjacent stitches is optional. Repeat rows: 1-8.

Knit through the back leg; purl as follows: with the working yarn in front of the stitch, insert the right needle through the stitch from back to front, move the working yarn under the right needle and pull it with the needle through the stitch. The purl stitch that is worked this way sets up the knit stitch to be knitted through the back leg.

Description:

Row 1: Purl 2, slip 6 onto a cable needle in the front of your work, knit the next 6, knit the slipped 6, knit the next 12, purl 2.

Row 2: Knit 2, purl 24, knit 2.

Row 3: Purl 2, knit 24, purl 2.

Row 4: Knit 2, purl 24, knit 2.

Row 5: Purl 2, knit 12, slip the next 6 onto a cable needle behind your work, knit the next 6, knit the slipped 6, purl 2.

Row 6: Knit 2, purl 24, knit 2.

Row 7: Purl 2, knit 24, purl 2.

Row 8: Knit 2, purl 24, knit 2.

Repeat rows: 1-8.

Bind off as follows: After the last row 1, turn your work over; the Back Side: slip all the stitches from the left needle to the right one, as a result, the working yarn is at the end of the row; turn your work over; the Front Side: slip 2 stitches from the left needle to the right one, insert the left needle through the 1st slipped stitch from left to right and pass it over the 2nd one; now there is 1 stitch on the right needle; *slip 1 from the left needle to the right one (now, there are 2 stitches on the right needle), insert the left needle from left to right through the 1st stitch on the right needle and pass it over the 2nd one (now, there is 1 stitch on the right needle)* repeat from * to * until the end of the row. Note: For trimming, bind off loosely using larger needles than the working ones, in order to create a larger chain of edge stitches, as this type of binding off creates a tight chain of small edge stitches that look already finished.

Pattern 15

Cast on a multiple of 12, plus 2 edge stitches. Twelve-stitch repeat. Repeat rows: 3-14. The edge stitches are not included in the description below and must be added. Slip the first edge stitch; purl the last edge stitch as if to purl in knitting through the back leg as follows: insert the right needle through the stitch from back to front, move the working yarn under the right needle, and pull it through the stitch.

Knit through the front leg, purl as follows: with the working yarn in front of the stitch, insert the right needle through the stitch from back to front and wrap the working yarn counterclockwise around the tip of the right needle, then pull the working yarn with the right needle through the stitch. The purl stitch that is worked this way sets up the knit stitch to be knitted through the front leg.

Description:

Row 1 (set up row): knit all the stitches.

Row 2 (set up row): purl 4, yarn over clockwise, purl 1, yarn over clockwise, purl 1, *purl 10, yarn over clockwise, purl 1, yarn over clockwise, purl 1* repeat from * to * until the end of the row before the edge stitch, purl the last 6.

Row 3: slip 6 onto a cable needle in front of your work, knit the next 1, slip the next yarn over of the previous row off the left needle and leave it as is, knit the next 1, slip the next yarn over of the previous row off the left needle and leave it as is, then knit the slipped 6, *knit 4, slip 6 onto a cable needle in front of your work, knit the next 1, slip the next yarn over of the previous row off the left needle and leave it as is, knit the next 1, slip the next yarn over of the previous row off the left needle and leave it as is, then knit the slipped 6* repeat from * to * until the end of the row before the edge stitch, knit the last 4.

Row 4: purl 2, yarn over clockwise, purl 1, yarn over clockwise, purl 1, purl 2, *purl 8, yarn over clockwise, purl 1, yarn over clockwise, purl 1, purl 2* repeat from * to * until the end of the row before the edge stitch, purl the last 6.

Row 5: knit 2, slip 6 onto a cable needle in front of your work, knit the next 1, slip the next yarn over of the previous row off the left needle and leave it as is, knit the next 1, slip the next yarn over of the previous row off the left needle and leave it as is, then knit the slipped 6, *knit 4, slip 6 onto a cable needle in front of your work, knit the next 1, slip the next yarn over of the previous row off the left needle and leave it as is, knit the next 1, slip the next yarn over of the previous row off the left needle and leave it as is, then knit the slipped 6* repeat from * to * until the end of the row before the edge stitch, knit the last 2.

Row 6: yarn over clockwise, purl 1, yarn over clockwise, purl 1, purl 4, *purl 6, yarn over clockwise, purl 1, yarn over clockwise, purl 1, purl 4* repeat from * to * until the end of the row before the edge stitch, purl the last 6.

Row 7: knit 4, *slip 6 onto a cable needle in front of your work, knit the next 1, slip the next yarn over of the previous row off the left needle and leave it as is, knit the next 1, slip the next yarn over of the previous row off the left needle and leave it as is, then knit the slipped 6, knit the next 4* repeat from * to * until the end of the row before the edge stitch—the last 8 stitches—slip 6 onto a cable needle in front of your work, knit the next 1, slip the next yarn over of the previous row off the left needle and leave it as is, knit the next 1, slip the next yarn over of the previous row off the left needle and leave it as is, then knit the slipped 6.

Row 8: purl 6, *purl 6, yarn over clockwise, purl 1, yarn over clockwise, purl 1, purl the next 4* repeat from * to * until the end of the row before the edge stitch, purl the last 6.

Row 9: knit 6, *knit 4, slip 1 onto a cable needle behind your work, slip the next yarn over of the previous row off the left needle and leave it as is, slip the next 1 onto a cable needle behind your work, slip the next yarn over of the previous row off the left needle and leave it as is, knit 6, then knit the slipped 2* repeat from * to * until the end of the row before the edge stitch, knit the last 6.

Row 10: purl 6, *purl 8, yarn over clockwise, purl 1, yarn over clockwise, purl 1, then purl 2* repeat from * to * until the end of the row before the edge stitch, purl the last 6.

Row 11: knit 6, *knit 2, slip 1 onto a cable needle behind your work, slip the next yarn over of the previous row off the left needle and leave it as is, slip the next 1 onto a cable needle behind your work, slip the next yarn over of the previous row off the left needle and leave it as is, knit the next 6, then knit the slipped 2, then knit the next 2* repeat from * to * until the end of the row before the edge stitch, knit the last 6.

Row 12: purl 6, *purl 10, yarn over clockwise, purl 1, yarn over clockwise, purl 1* repeat from * to * until the end of the row before the edge stitch, purl the last 6.

Row 13: knit 6, *slip 1 onto a cable needle behind your work, slip the next yarn over of the previous row off the left needle and leave it as is, slip the next 1 onto a cable needle behind your work, slip the next yarn over of the previous row off the left needle and leave it as is, knit the next 6, then knit the slipped 2, then knit the next 4* repeat from * to * until the end of the row before the edge stitch, knit the last 6.

Row 14: purl 4, yarn over clockwise, purl 1, yarn over clockwise, purl 1, *purl 10, yarn over clockwise, purl 1, yarn over clockwise, purl 1* repeat from * to * until the end of the row before the edge stitch, purl the last 6.

Repeat rows: 3-14.

Bind off as follows: After the last row 13, turn your work over; the Back Side: slip all the stitches from the left needle to the right one, as a result, the working yarn is at the end of the row; turn your work over; the Front Side: slip 2 stitches from the left needle to the right one, insert the left needle through the 1st slipped stitch from left to right and pass it over the 2nd one (now, there is 1 stitch on the right needle); *slip 1 from the left needle to the right one, now there are 2 stitches on the right needle, insert the left needle from left to right through the 1st stitch on the right needle and pass it over the 2nd one (now, there is 1 stitch on the right needle)* repeat from * to * until the end of the row. Note: For trimming, bind off loosely using larger needles than the working ones, in order to create a larger chain of edge stitches, as this type of binding off creates a tight chain of small edge stitches that look already finished.

Pattern 16

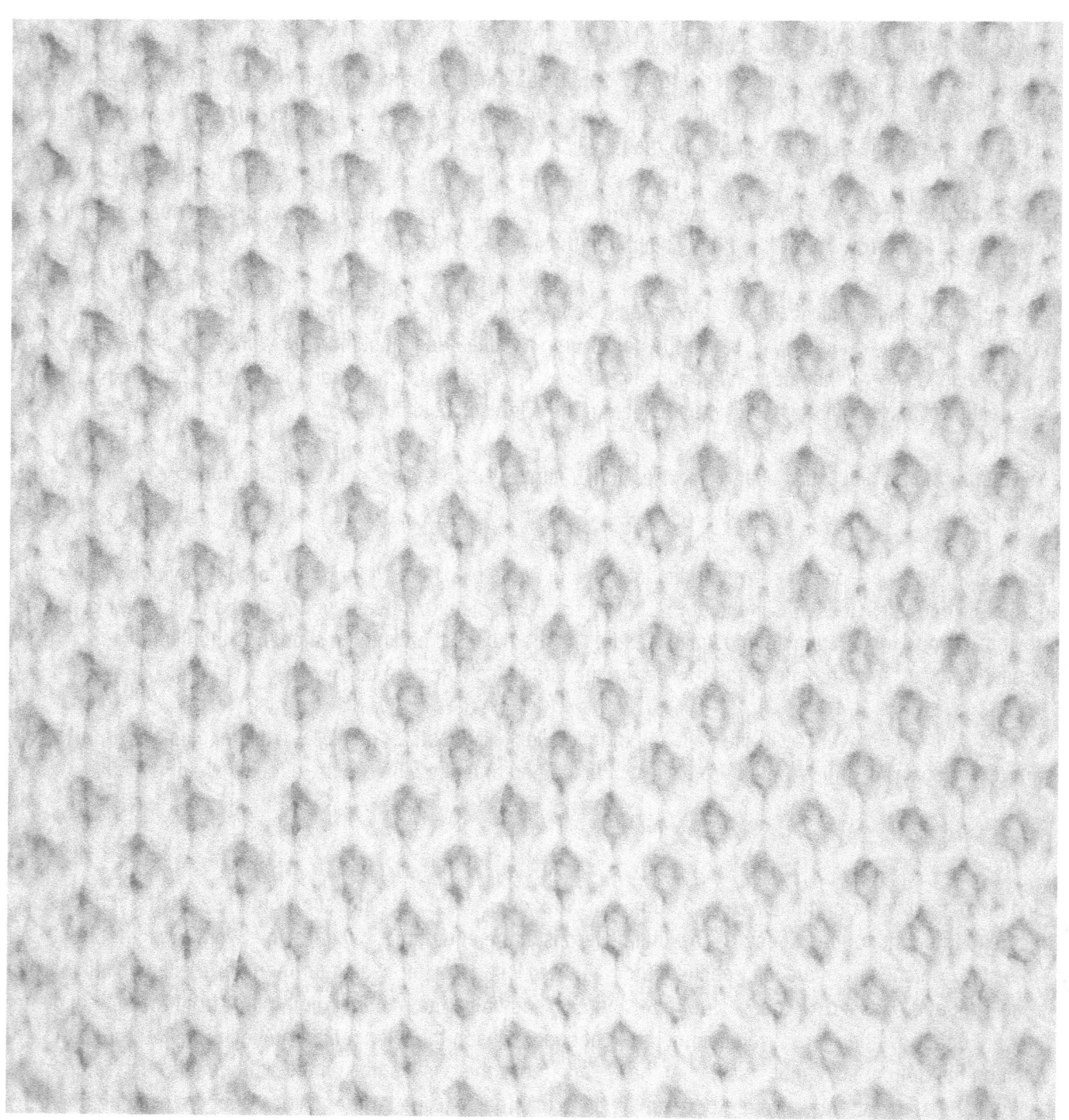

Cast on a multiple of 4, plus 2 edge stitches. Four-stitch repeat. Repeat rows: 1-4. The edge stitches are not included in the description below and must be added. Slip the first edge stitch; purl the last edge stitch.

Knit through the back leg, purl as if to purl in knitting through the back leg follows: with the working yarn in front of the stitch, insert the right needle through the stitch from back to front, move the right needle under the right needle and pull it through the stitch. The purl stitch that is worked this way sets up the knit stitch to be worked through the back leg.

Description:

Row 1: *Knit 2 as follows: swap 2 on the left needle, inserting the right needle in front of your work through the 2nd stitch purlwise and slipping both stitches off the left needle, then pick up the 1st stitch onto the left needle, inserting the left needle through the 1st stitch straight, behind the 2nd stitch, then slip the 2nd stitch from the right needle to the left one, thus the 2nd stitch becomes the 1st one, now knit each stitch through the back leg, knit the next 2 as follows: knit the 2nd stitch through the back leg, then knit the 1st stitch through the back leg* repeat from * to * until the end of the row.

Row 2: Purl all the stitches.

Row 3: *Knit 2 as follows: knit the 2nd stitch through the back leg, then knit the 1st stitch through the back leg, knit the next 2 as follows: swap the 2nd and the 1st stitches on the left needle, inserting the right needle in front of your work through the 2nd stitch purlwise and slipping both stitches off the left needle, then pick up the 1st stitch onto the left needle straight, behind the 2nd stitch, then slip the 2nd stitch from the right needle to the left one, thus the 2nd stitch becomes the 1st one, now knit each stitch through the back leg* repeat from * to * until the end of the row.

Row 4: Purl all the stitches.

Repeat rows: 1-4.

Bind off as follows: After the last row 3, turn your work over; the Back Side: slip all the stitches from the left needle to the right one, as a result, the working yarn is at the end of the row; turn your work over; the Front Side: slip 2 stitches from the left needle to the right one, insert the left needle through the 1st slipped stitch from left to right and pass it over the 2nd one (now, there is 1 stitch on the right needle); *slip 1 from the left needle to the right one, now there are 2 stitches on the right needle, insert the left needle from left to right through the 1st stitch on the right needle and pass it over the 2nd one (now, there is 1 stitch on the right needle)* repeat from * to * until the end of the row.

Note: For trimming, bind off loosely using larger needles than the working ones, in order to create a larger chain of edge stitches, as this type of binding off creates a tight chain of small edge stitches that look already finished.

Pattern 17

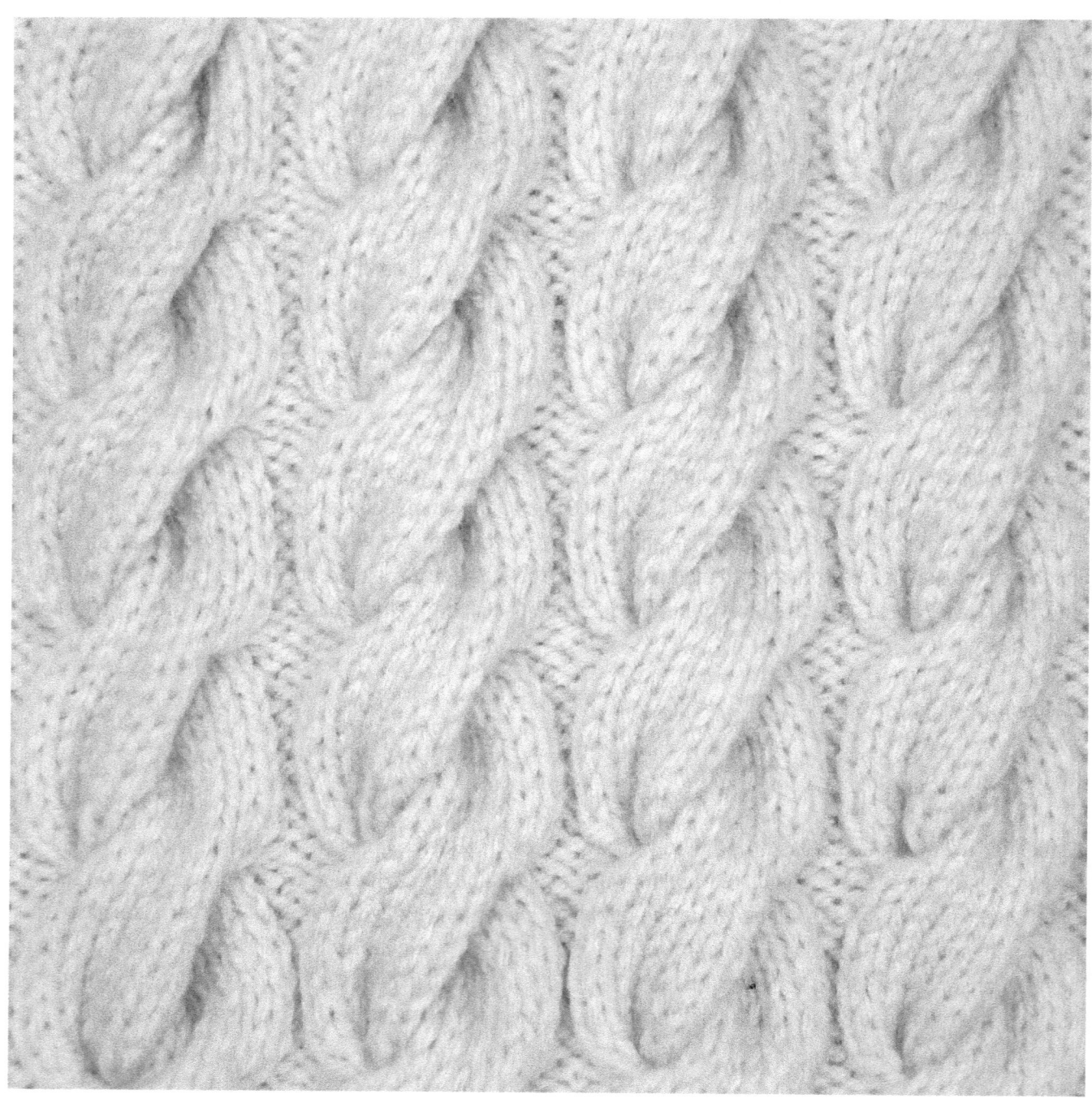

Cast on a multiple of 19, plus 3 for symmetry, and plus 2 edge stitches. Nineteen-stitch repeat. Repeat rows: 1-10. The edge stitches are not included in the description below and must be added. Slip the first edge stitch; purl the last edge stitch.

Knit through the back leg, purl as if to purl in knitting through the back leg follows: with the working yarn in front of the stitch, insert the right needle through the stitch from back to front, move the right needle under the right needle and pull it through the stitch. The purl stitch that is worked this way sets up the knit stitch to be worked through the back leg.

Description:

Row 1: *Purl 3, slip 8 onto a cable needle behind your work, knit the next 8, then knit the slipped 8* repeat from * to * until the end of the row before the edge stitch, purl 3.

Row 2: *Knit 3, purl 16* repeat from * to * until the end of the row before the edge stitch, knit 3.

Row 3: *Purl 3, knit 16* repeat from * to * until the end of the row before the edge stitch, purl 3.

Row 4: *Knit 3, purl 16* repeat from * to * until the end of the row before the edge stitch, knit 3.

Row 5: *Purl 3, knit 16* repeat from * to * until the end of the row before the edge stitch, purl 3.

Row 6: *Knit 3, purl 16 * repeat from * to * until the end of the row before the edge stitch, knit 3.

Row 7: *Purl 3, knit 16 * repeat from * to * until the end of the row before the edge stitch, purl 3.

Row 8: *Knit 3, purl 16 * repeat from * to * until the end of the row before the edge stitch, knit 3.

Row 9: *Purl 3, knit 16 * repeat from * to * until the end of the row before the edge stitch, purl 3.

Row 10: *Knit 3, purl 16 * repeat from * to * until the end of the row before the edge stitch, knit 3.

Repeat rows: 1-10.

Bind off as follows: After the last row 1, turn your work over; the Back Side: slip all the stitches from the left needle to the right one, as a result, the working yarn is at the end of the row; turn your work over; the Front Side: slip 2 stitches from the left needle to the right one, insert the left needle through the 1st slipped stitch from left to right and pass it over the 2nd one (now, there is 1 stitch on the right needle); *slip 1 from the left needle to the right one (now there are 2 stitches on the right needle), insert the left needle through the 1st stitch on the right needle from left to right and pass it over the 2nd one (now, there is 1 stitch on the right needle)* repeat from * to * until the end of the row. Note: For trimming, bind off loosely using larger needles than the working ones, in order to create a larger chain of edge stitches, as this type of binding off creates a tight chain of small edge stitches that look already finished.

Pattern 18

Cast on 20

stitches for the braid, plus 4 adjacent stitches (2 at each side of the braid). The number of adjacent stitches are optional. Repeat rows: 1-8.

Knit through the back leg, purl as if to purl in knitting through the back leg follows: with the working yarn in front of the stitch, insert the right needle through the stitch from back to front, move the right needle under the right needle and pull it through the stitch. The purl stitch that is worked this way sets up the knit stitch to be worked through the back leg.

Description:

Row 1: Purl 2, knit 4, slip the next 4 onto a cable needle in front of your work, knit the next 4, knit the slipped 4, slip the next 4 onto a cable needle in front of your work, knit the next 4, knit the slipped 4, purl 2.

Row 2: Knit 2, purl 20, knit 2.

Row 3: Purl 2, knit 20, purl 2.

Row 4: Knit 2, purl 20, knit 2.

Row 5: Purl 2, slip 4 onto a cable needle behind your work, knit the next 4, knit the slipped 4, slip the next 4 onto a cable needle behind your work, knit the next 4, knit the slipped 4, knit 4, purl 2.

Row 6: Knit 2, purl 20, knit 2.

Row 7: Purl 2, knit 20, purl 2.

Row 8: Knit 2, purl 20, knit 2.

Repeat rows: 1-8.

Bind off as follows: After the last row 1, turn your work over; the Back Side: slip all the stitches from the left needle to the right one, as a result, the working yarn is at the end of the row; turn your work over; the Front Side: slip 2 purlwise from the left needle to the right one, insert the left needle from left to right through the 1st slipped stitch and pass it over the 2nd stitch (now, there is 1 stitch on the right needle); *slip 1 purlwise from the left needle to the right one, insert the left needle from left to right through the 1st stitch on the right needle and pass it over the 2nd stitch (now, there is 1 stitch on the right needle)* repeat from * to * until the end of the row.

Note: For trimming, bind off loosely using larger needles than the working ones, in order to create a larger chain of edge stitches, as this type of binding off creates a tight chain of small edge stitches that look already finished.

Pattern 19

Cast on 32 stitches for the braid, plus 6 adjacent stitches (3 at each side of the braid). The number of adjacent stitches is optional. Repeat rows: 1-6. The edge stitches are not included in the description below and must be added. Slip the first edge stitch; purl the last edge stitch.

Knit through the back leg, purl as to purl in knitting through the back leg follows: with the working yarn in front of the stitch, insert the right needle through the stitch from back to front, move the working yarn under the right needle and pull it through the stitch. The purl stitch that is worked this way sets up the knit stitch to be knitted through the back leg.

Description:

Row 1: purl 3, knit 8, slip 4 onto a cable needle behind your work, knit the next 4, then knit the slipped 4, slip the next 4 onto a cable needle in front of your work, knit the next 4, then knit the slipped 4, knit the next 8, purl 3.

Row 2: knit 3, purl 32, knit 3.

Row 3: purl 3, knit 4, slip the next 4 onto a cable needle behind your work, knit the next 4, then knit the slipped 4, knit the next 8, slip the next 4 onto a cable needle in front of your work, knit the next 4, then knit the slipped 4, knit the next 4, purl 3.

Row 4: knit 3, purl 32, knit 3.

Row 5: purl 3, slip 4 onto a cable needle behind your work, knit the next 4, then knit the slipped 4, knit the next 16, slip the next 4 onto a cable needle in front of your work, knit the next 4, then knit the slipped 4, purl 3.

Row 6: knit 3, purl 32, knit 3.

Repeat rows: 1-6.

Bind off as follows: After the last row 5, turn your work over; the Back Side: slip all the stitches from the left needle to the right one, now the working yarn is at the end of the row; turn your work over; the Front Side: slip 2 purlwise from the left needle to the right one, insert the left needle from left to right through the 1st slipped stitch and pass it over the 2nd stitch (now, there is 1 stitch on the right needle); *slip 1 purlwise from the left needle to the right one, insert the left needle from left to right through the 1st stitch on the right needle and pass it over the 2nd stitch (now, there is 1 stitch on the right needle)* repeat from * to * until the end of the row.

Note: For trimming, bind off loosely using larger needles than the working ones, in order to create a larger chain of edge stitches, as this type of binding off creates a tight chain of small edge stitches that look already finished.

Pattern 20

Cast on a multiple of 11, plus 2 for symmetry, and plus 2 edge stitches. Eleven-stitch repeat. Repeat rows: 1-4. The edge stitches are not included in the description below and must be added. Slip the first edge stitch; purl the last edge stitch.

Knit through the back leg, purl as follows: with the working yarn in front of the stitch, insert the right needle through the stitch from back to front, move the working yarn under the right needle and pull it through the stitch. The purl stitch that is worked this way sets up the knit stitch to be knitted through the back leg.

Description:

Row 1: *Purl 2, slip 3 onto a cable needle in front of your work, knit the next 3, then knit the slipped 3, knit 3* repeat from * to * until the end of the row before the edge stitch, purl 2.

Row 2: *Knit 2, purl 9* repeat from * to * until the end of the row before the edge stitch, knit 2.

Row 3: *Purl 2, knit 3, slip the next 3 onto a cable needle behind your work, knit the next 3, then knit the slipped 3* repeat from * to * until the end of the row before the edge stitch, purl 2.

Row 4: *Knit 2, purl 9* repeat from * to * until the end of the row before the edge stitch, knit 2.

Repeat rows: 1-4.

Bind off as follows: After the last row 3, turn your work over; the Back Side: slip all the stitches from the left needle to the right one, now the working yarn is at the end of the row; turn your work over; the Front Side: slip 2 purlwise from the left needle to the right one, insert the left needle from left to right through the 1st slipped stitch and pass it over the 2nd stitch (now, there is 1 stitch on the right needle); *slip 1 purlwise from the left needle to the right one, insert the left needle from left to right through the 1st stitch on the right needle and pass it over the 2nd stitch (now, there is 1 stitch on the right needle)* repeat from * to * until the end of the row.

Note: For trimming, bind off loosely using larger needles than the working ones, in order to create a larger chain of edge stitches, as this type of binding off creates a tight chain of small edge stitches that look already finished.

Pattern 21

Cast on a multiple of 27, plus 3 for symmetry, and plus 2 edge stitches. Twenty-seven-stitch repeat. Repeat rows: 1-6. The edge stitches are not included in the description below and must be added. Slip the first edge stitch; purl the last edge stitch.

Knit through the back leg, purl as follows: with the working yarn in front of the stitch, insert the right needle through the stitch from back to front, move the working yarn under the right needle and pull it through the stitch. The purl stitch that is worked this way sets up the knit stitch to be knitted through the back leg.

Description:

Row 1: *purl 3, knit 6, slip 3 onto a cable needle behind your work, knit the next 3, then knit the slipped 3, slip the next 3 onto a cable needle in front of your work, knit the next 3, then knit the slipped 3, knit the next 6* repeat from * to * until the end of the row before the edge stitch, purl 3.

Row 2: *knit 3, purl 24* repeat from * to * until the end of the row before the edge stitch, knit 3.

Row 3: *purl 3, knit 3, slip the next 3 onto a cable needle behind your work, knit the next 3, then knit the slipped 3, knit the next 6, slip the next 3 onto a cable needle in front of your work, knit the next 3, then knit the slipped 3, knit the next 3* repeat from * to * until the end of the row before the edge stitch, purl 3.

Row 4: *knit 3, purl 24* repeat from * to * until the end of the row before the edge stitch, knit 3.

Row 5: *purl 3, slip 3 onto a cable needle behind your work, knit the next 3, then knit the slipped 3, knit the next 12, slip the next 3 onto a cable needle in front of your work, knit the next 3, then knit the slipped 3* repeat from * to * until the end of the row before the edge stitch, purl 3.

Row 6: *knit 3, purl 24* repeat from * to * until the end of the row before the edge stitch, knit 3.

Repeat rows: 1-6.

Bind off as follows: After the last row 5, turn your work over; the Back Side: slip all the stitches from the left needle to the right one, now the working yarn is at the end of the row; turn your work over; the Front Side: slip 2 purlwise from the left needle to the right one, insert the left needle from left to right through the 1st slipped stitch and pass it over the 2nd stitch (now, there is 1 stitch on the right needle); *slip 1 purlwise from the left needle to the right one, insert the left needle from left to right through the 1st stitch on the right needle and pass it over the 2nd stitch (now, there is 1 stitch on the right needle)* repeat from * to * until the end of the row.

Note: For trimming, bind off loosely using larger needles than the working ones, in order to create a larger chain of edge stitches, as this type of binding off creates a tight chain of small edge stitches that look already finished.

Pattern 22

Cast on a multiple of 20, plus 2 for symmetry, and plus 2 edge stitches. Twenty-stitch repeat. Repeat rows: 1-8. The edge stitches are not included in the description below and must be added. Slip the first edge stitch; purl the last edge stitch.

Knit through the back leg, purl as follows: with the working yarn in front of the stitch, insert the right needle through the stitch from back to front, move the working yarn under the right needle and pull it through the stitch. The purl stitch that is worked this way sets up the knit stitch to be knitted through the back leg.

Description:

Row 1: *Purl 2, knit 18* repeat from * to * until the end of the row before the edge stitch, purl 2.

Row 2: *Knit 2, purl 18* repeat from * to * until the end of the row before the edge stitch, knit 2.

Row 3: *Purl 2, slip 6 onto a cable needle in front of your work, knit the next 6, knit the slipped 6, knit the next 6* repeat from * to * until the end of the row before the edge stitch, purl 2.

Row 4: *Knit 2, purl 18* repeat from * to * until the end of the row before the edge stitch, knit 2.

Row 5: *Purl 2, knit 18* repeat from * to * until the end of the row before the edge stitch, purl 2.

Row 6: *Knit 2, purl 18* repeat from * to * until the end of the row before the edge stitch, knit 2.

Row 7: *Purl 2, knit 6, slip the next 6 onto a cable needle behind your work, knit the next 6, knit the slipped 6* repeat from * to * until the end of the row before the edge stitch, purl 2.

Row 8: *Knit 2, purl 18* repeat from * to * until the end of the row before the edge stitch, knit 2.

Repeat rows: 1-8.

Bind off as follows: After the last row 7, turn your work over; the Back Side: slip all the stitches from the left needle to the right one, now the working yarn is at the end of the row; turn your work over; the Front Side: slip 2 purlwise from the left needle to the right one, insert the left needle from left to right through the 1st slipped stitch and pass it over the 2nd stitch (now, there is 1 stitch on the right needle); *slip 1 purlwise from the left needle to the right one, insert the left needle from left to right through the 1st stitch on the right needle and pass it over the 2nd stitch (now, there is 1 stitch on the right needle)* repeat from * to * until the end of the row.

Note: For trimming, bind off loosely using larger needles than the working ones, in order to create a larger chain of edge stitches, as this type of binding off creates a tight chain of small edge stitches that look already finished.

Pattern 23

Cast on a multiple of 33, plus 3 for symmetry, and plus 2 edge stitches. Thirty-three-stitch repeat. Repeat rows: 1-12. The edge stitches are not included in the description below and must be added. Slip the first edge stitch; purl the last edge stitch.

Knit through the back leg, purl as follows: with the working yarn in front of the stitch, insert the right needle through the stitch from back to front, move the working yarn under the right needle and pull it through the stitch. The purl stitch that is worked this way sets up the knit stitch to be knitted through the back leg.

Description:

Row 1: *Purl 3, knit 30* repeat from * to * until the end of the row before the edge stitch, purl 3.

Row 2: *Knit 3, purl 30* repeat from * to * until the end of the row before the edge stitch, knit 3.

Row 3: *Purl 3, slip 10 onto a cable needle in front of your work, knit the next 10, then knit the slipped 10, knit the next 10* repeat from * to * until the end of the row before the edge stitch, purl 3.

Row 4: *Knit 3, purl 30* repeat from * to * until the end of the row before the edge stitch, knit 3.

Row 5: *Purl 3, knit 30* repeat from * to * until the end of the row before the edge stitch, purl 3.

Row 6: *Knit 3, purl 30* repeat from * to * until the end of the row before the edge stitch, knit 3.

Row 7: *Purl 3, knit 30* repeat from * to * until the end of the row before the edge stitch, purl 3.

Row 8: *Knit 3, purl 30* repeat from * to * until the end of the row before the edge stitch, knit 3.

Row 9: *Purl 3, knit 10, slip the next 10 onto a cable needle behind your work, knit the next 10, then knit the slipped 10* repeat from * to * until the end of the row before the edge stitch, purl 3.

Row 10: *Knit 3, purl 30* repeat from * to * until the end of the row before the edge stitch, knit 3.

Row 11: *Purl 3, knit 30* repeat from * to * until the end of the row before the edge stitch, purl 3.

Row 12: *Knit 3, purl 30* repeat from * to * until the end of the row before the edge stitch, knit 3.

Repeat rows: 1-12.

Bind off as follows: After the last row 3, turn your work over; the Back Side: slip all the stitches from the left needle to the right one, now the working yarn is at the end of the row; turn your work over; the Front Side: slip 2 purlwise from the left needle to the right one, insert the left needle from left to right through the 1st slipped stitch and pass it over the 2nd stitch (now, there is 1 stitch on the right needle); *slip 1 purlwise from the left needle to the right one, insert the left needle from left to right through the 1st stitch on the right needle and pass it over the

2nd stitch (now, there is 1 stitch on the right needle)* repeat from * to * until the end of the row.

Note: For trimming, bind off loosely using larger needles than the working ones, in order to create a larger chain of edge stitches, as this type of binding off creates a tight chain of small edge stitches that look already finished.

Pattern 24

Cast on a multiple of 15, plus 3 for symmetry, and plus 2 edge stitches. Fifteen-stitch-repeat. Repeat rows: 1-12. The edge stitches are not included in the description below and must be added. Slip the first edge stitch; purl the last edge stitch. Knit through the back leg, purl as follows: with the working yarn in front of the stitch, insert the right needle through the stitch from back to front, move the working yarn under the right needle and pull it through the stitch.

Description:

Row 1: *Purl 3, slip 4 onto a cable needle in front of your work, knit the next 4, knit the slipped 4, knit the next 4* repeat from * to * until the end of the row before the edge stitch, purl 3.

Row 2: *Knit 3, purl 12* repeat from * to * until the end of the row before the edge stitch, knit 3.

Row 3: *Purl 3, knit 12* repeat from * to * until the end of the row before the edge stitch, purl 3.

Row 4: *Knit 3, purl 12* repeat from * to * until the end of the row before the edge stitch, knit 3.

Row 5: *Purl 3, knit 12* repeat from * to * until the end of the row before the edge stitch, purl 3.

Row 6: *Knit 3, purl 12* repeat from * to * until the end of the row before the edge stitch, knit 3.

Row 7: *Purl 3, knit 4, slip the next 4 onto a cable needle behind your work, knit the next 4, knit the slipped 4* repeat from * to * until the end of the row before the edge stitch, purl 3.

Row 8: *Knit 3, purl 12* repeat from * to * until the end of the row before the edge stitch, knit 3.

Row 9: *Purl 3, knit 12* repeat from * to * until the end of the row before the edge stitch, purl 3.

Row 10: *Knit 3, purl 12* repeat from * to * until the end of the row before the edge stitch, knit 3.

Row 11: *Purl 3, knit 12* repeat from * to * until the end of the row before the edge stitch, purl 3.

Row 12: *Knit 3, purl 12* repeat from * to * until the end of the row before the edge stitch, knit 3.

Repeat rows: 1-12.

Bind off as follows: After the last row 1, turn your work over; the Back Side: slip all the stitches from the left needle to the right one, now the working yarn is at the end of the row; turn your work over; the Front Side: slip 2 purlwise from the left needle to the right one, insert the left needle from left to right through the 1st slipped stitch and pass it over the 2nd stitch (now, there is 1 stitch on the right needle); *slip 1 purlwise from the left needle to the right one, insert the left needle from left to right through the 1st stitch on the right needle and pass it over the 2nd stitch (now, there is 1 stitch on the right needle)* repeat from * to * until the end of the row.

Note: For trimming, bind off loosely using larger needles than the working ones, in order to create a larger chain of edge stitches, as this type of binding off creates a tight chain of small edge stitches that look already finished.

Pattern 25

Cast on a multiple of 24, plus 4 for symmetry, and plus 2 edge stitches. Twenty-four- stitch repeat. Repeat rows: 1-12. The edge stitches are not included in the description below and must be added. Slip the first edge stitch; purl the last edge stitch. Knit through the back leg, purl as follows: with the working yarn in front of the stitch, insert the right needle through the stitch from back to front, move the working yarn under the right needle and pull it through the stitch.

Description:

Row 1: *Purl 4, knit 20* repeat from * to * until the end of the row before the edge stitch, purl 4.

Row 2: *Knit 4, purl 20* repeat from * to * until the end of the row before the edge stitch, knit 4.

Row 3: *Purl 4, slip 10 onto a cable needle behind your work, knit the next 10, knit the slipped 10* repeat from * to * until the end of the row before the edge stitch, purl 4.

Row 4: *Knit 4, purl 20* repeat from * to * until the end of the row before the edge stitch, knit 4.

Row 5: *Purl 4, knit 20* repeat from * to * until the end of the row before the edge stitch, purl 4.

Row 6: *Knit 4, purl 20* repeat from * to * until the end of the row before the edge stitch, knit 4.

Row 7: *Purl 4, knit 20* repeat from * to * until the end of the row before the edge stitch, purl 4.

Row 8: *Knit 4, purl 20* repeat from * to * until the end of the row before the edge stitch, knit 4.

Row 9: *Purl 4, knit 20* repeat from * to * until the end of the row before the edge stitch, purl 4.

Row 10: *Knit 4, purl 20* repeat from * to * until the end of the row before the edge stitch, knit 4.

Row 11: *Purl 4, knit 20* repeat from * to * until the end of the row before the edge stitch, purl 4.

Row 12: *Knit 4, purl 20* repeat from * to * until the end of the row before the edge stitch, knit 4.

Repeat rows: 1-12.

Bind off as follows: After the last row 5, turn your work over; the Back Side: slip all the stitches from the left needle to the right one, now the working yarn is at the end of the row; turn your work over; the Front Side: slip 2 purlwise from the left needle to the right one, insert the left needle from left to right through the 1st slipped stitch and pass it over the 2nd stitch (now, there is 1 stitch on the right needle), *slip 1 purlwise from the left needle to the right one, insert the left needle from left to right through the 1st stitch on the right needle and pass it over the 2nd stitch (now, there is 1 stitch on the right needle)* repeat from * to * until the end of the row.

Note: For trimming, bind off loosely using larger needles than the working ones, in order to create a larger chain of edge stitches, as this type of binding off creates a tight chain of small edge stitches that look already finished.

Pattern 26

Cast on a multiple of 8, plus 2 for symmetry, and plus 2 edge stitches. Eight-stitch repeat. Repeat rows: 1-4. The edge stitches are not included in the description below and must be added. Slip the first edge stitch; purl the last edge stitch.

Knit through the back leg, purl as follows: with the working yarn in front of the stitch, insert the right needle through the stitch from back to front, move the working yarn under the right needle and pull it through the stitch. The purl stitch that is worked this way sets up the knit stitch to be knitted through the back leg.

Description:

Row 1: *Purl 2, slip 3 onto a cable needle behind your work, knit the next 3, then knit the slipped 3* repeat from * to * before the edge stitch, purl 2.

Row 2: *Knit 2, purl 6* repeat from * to * until the end of the row before the edge stitch, knit 2.

Row 3: *Purl 2, knit 6* repeat from * to * until the end of the row before the edge stitch, purl 2.

Row 4: *Knit 2, purl 6* repeat from * to * until the end of the row before the edge stitch, knit 2.

Repeat rows: 1-4.

Bind off as follows: After the last row 1, turn your work over; the Back Side: slip all the stitches from the left needle to the right one, now the working yarn is at the end of the row; turn your work over; the Front Side: slip 2 purlwise from the left needle to the right one, insert the left needle from left to right through the 1st slipped stitch and pass it over the 2nd stitch (now, there is 1 stitch on the right needle); *slip 1 purlwise from the left needle to the right one, insert the left needle from left to right through the 1st stitch on the right needle and pass it over the 2nd stitch (now, there is 1 stitch on the right needle)* repeat from * to * until the end of the row.

Note: For trimming, bind off loosely using larger needles than the working ones, in order to create a larger chain of edge stitches, as this type of binding off creates a tight chain of small edge stitches that look already finished.

Pattern 27

Cast on a multiple of 25, plus 4 for symmetry, and plus 2 edge stitches.
Twenty-five-stitch repeat. Repeat rows: 1-12. The edge stitches are not included in the description below and must be added. Slip the first edge stitch; purl the last edge stitch.

Knit through the back leg, purl as follows: with the working yarn in front of the stitch, insert the right needle through the stitch from back to front, move the working yarn under the right needle and pull it through the stitch. The purl stitch that is worked this way sets up the knit stitch to be knitted through the back leg.

Description:

Row 1: *Purl 4, knit 21* repeat from * to * until the end of the row before the edge stitch, purl 4.

Row 2: *Knit 4, purl 21* repeat from * to * until the end of the row before the edge stitch, knit 4.

Row 3: *Purl 4, knit 6, slip the next 6 onto a cable needle behind your work, knit 9, knit the slipped 6* repeat from * to * until the end of the row before the edge stitch, purl 4.

Row 4: *Knit 4, purl 21* repeat from * to * until the end of the row before the edge stitch, knit 4.

Row 5: *Purl 4, knit 21* repeat from * to * until the end of the row before the edge stitch, purl 4.

Row 6: *Knit 4, purl 21* repeat from * to * until the end of the row before the edge stitch, knit 4.

Row 7: *Purl 4, knit 21* repeat from * to * until the end of the row before the edge stitch, purl 4.

Row 8: *Knit 4, purl 21* repeat from * to * until the end of the row before the edge stitch, knit 4.

Row 9: *Purl 4, slip 9 onto a cable needle in front of your work, knit the next 6, knit the slipped 9, knit 6* repeat from * to * until the end of the row before the edge stitch, purl 4.

Row 10: *Knit 4, purl 21* repeat from * to * until the end of the row before the edge stitch, knit 4.

Row 11: *Purl 4, knit 21* repeat from * to * until the end of the row before the edge stitch, purl 4.

Row 12: *Knit 4, purl 21* repeat from * to * until the end of the row before the edge stitch, knit 4.

Repeat rows: 1-12.

Bind off as follows: After the last row 9, turn your work over; the Back Side: slip all the stitches from the left needle to the right one, now the working yarn is at the end of the row; turn your work over; the Front Side: slip 2 purlwise from the left needle to the right one, insert the left needle from left to right through the 1st slipped stitch and pass it over the 2nd stitch (now, there is 1 stitch on the right needle); *slip 1 purlwise from the left needle to the right one, insert the left needle from left to right through the 1st stitch on the right needle and pass it over the 2nd stitch (now, there is 1 stitch on the right needle)* repeat from * to * until the end of the row.

Pattern 28

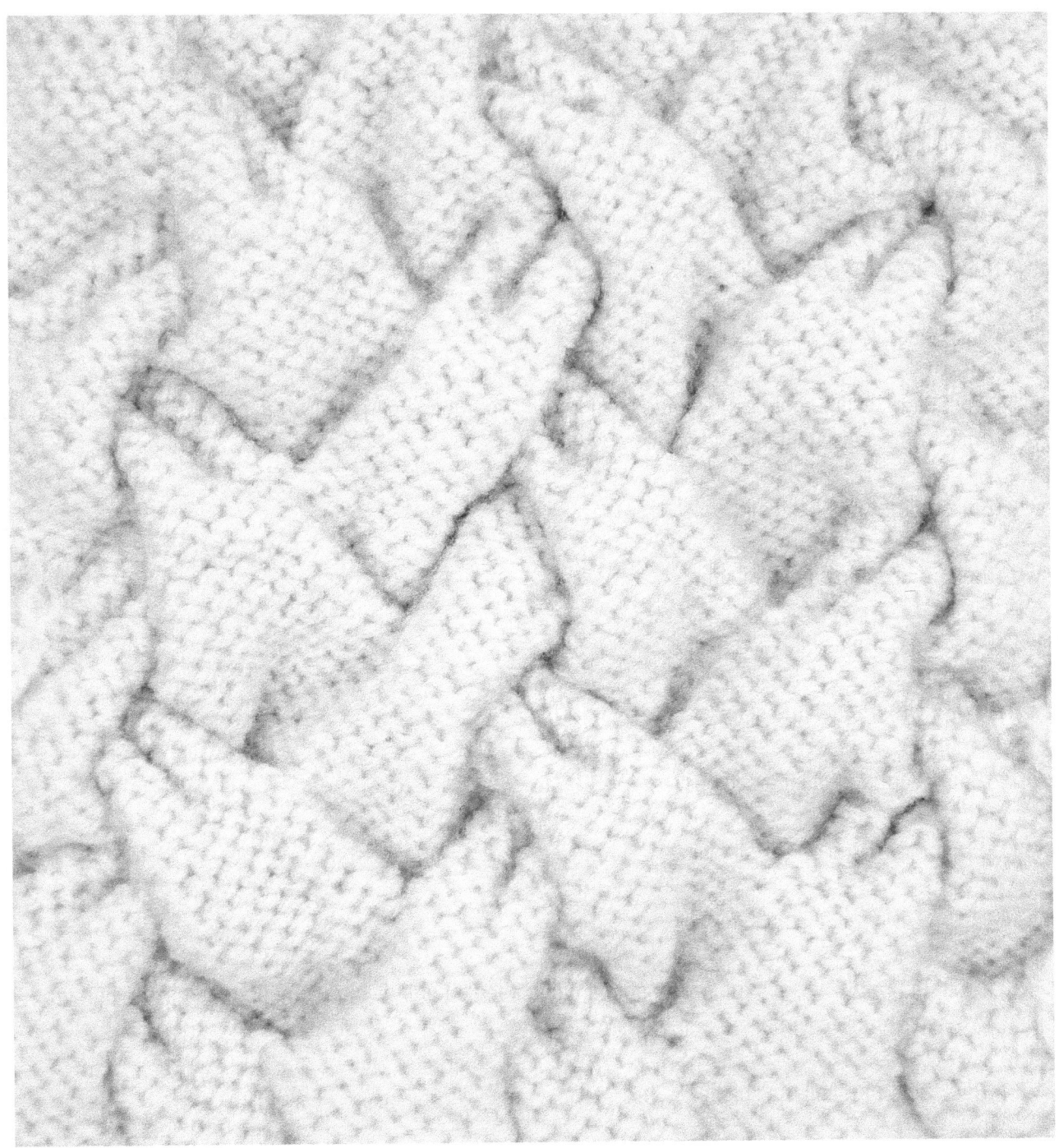

Cast on a multiple of 24, plus 2 edge stitches. Twenty-four-stitch repeat. Repeat rows: 1-16. The edge stitches are not included in the description below and must be added. Slip the first edge stitch; purl the last edge stitch.

Knit through the back leg, purl as follows: with the working yarn in front of the stitch, insert the right needle through the stitch from back to front, move the working yarn under the right needle and pull it through the stitch. The purl stitch that is worked this way sets up the knit stitch to be knitted through the back leg.

Description:

Row 1 (Front Side): Purl all the stitches.

Row 2 (Back Side): Knit all the stitches.

Row 3 (Front Side): Purl all the stitches.

Row 4 (Back Side): Knit all the stitches.

Row 5 (Front Side): *Slip 8 onto a cable needle in front of your work, purl the next 8, purl the slipped 8, purl the next 8* repeat from * to * until the end of the row.

Row 6 (Back Side): Knit all the stitches.

Row 7 (Front Side): Purl all the stitches.

Row 8 (Back Side): Knit all the stitches.

Row 9 (Front Side): Purl all the stitches.

Row 10 (Back Side): Knit all the stitches.

Row 11 (Front Side): Purl all the stitches.

Row 12 (Back Side): Knit all the stitches.

Row 13 (Front Side): *Purl 8, slip the next 8 onto a cable needle behind your work, purl the next 8, purl the slipped 8* repeat from * to * until the end of the row.

Row 14 (Back Side): Knit all the stitches.

Row 15 (Front Side): Purl all the stitches.

Row 16 (Back Side): Knit all the stitches.

Repeat rows: 1-16.

Bind off as follows: After the last row 13, turn your work over; the Back Side: slip all the stitches from the left needle to the right one; now the working yarn is at the end of the row; turn your work over; the Front Side: slip 2 purlwise from the left needle to the right one, insert the left needle from left to right through the 1st slipped stitch and pass it over the 2nd stitch (now, there is 1 stitch on the right needle); *slip 1 purlwise from the left needle to the right one, insert the left needle from left to right through the 1st stitch on the right needle and pass it over the 2nd stitch (now, there is 1 stitch on the right needle)* repeat from * to * until the end of the row.

Note: For trimming, bind off loosely using larger needles than the working ones, in order to create a larger chain of edge stitches, as this type of binding off creates a tight chain of small edge stitches that look already finished.

Pattern 29

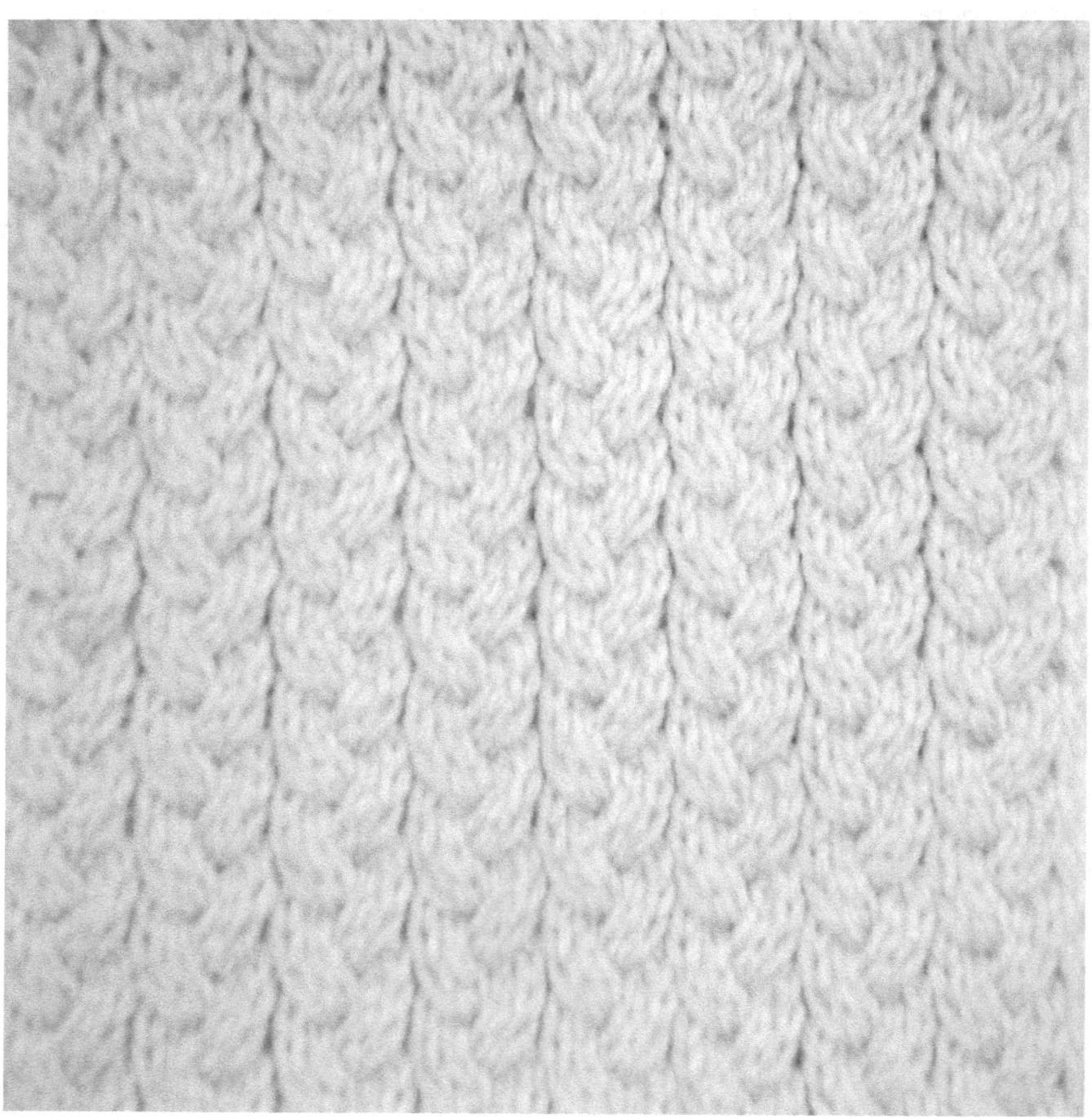

Cast on a multiple of 7, plus 1 for symmetry, and plus 2 edge stitches. Seven-stitch repeat. Repeat rows: 1-4. The edge stitches are not included in the description below and must be added. Slip the first edge stitch; purl the last edge stitch.

Knit through the back leg, purl as follows: with the working yarn in front of the stitch, insert the right needle through the stitch from back to front, move the working yarn under the right needle and pull it through the stitch. The purl stitch that is worked this way sets up the knit stitch to be knitted through the back leg.

Description:

Row 1: *Purl 1, slip the next 2 onto a cable needle behind your work, knit the next 2, then knit the slipped 2, knit the next 2* repeat from * to * until the end of the row before the edge stitch, purl 1.

Row 2: *Knit 1, purl 6* repeat from * to * until the end of the row before the edge stitch, knit 1.

Row 3: *Purl 1, knit 2, slip the next 2 onto a cable needle in front of your work, knit the next 2, then knit the slipped 2* repeat from * to * until the end of the row before the edge stitch, purl 1.

Row 4: *Knit 1, purl 6* repeat from * to * until the end of the row before the edge stitch, knit 1.

Repeat rows: 1-4.

Bind off as follows: After the last row 3, turn your work over; the Back Side: slip all the stitches from the left needle to the right one; now the working yarn is at the end of the row; turn your work over; the Front Side: slip 2 purlwise from the left needle to the right one, insert the left needle from left to right through the 1st slipped stitch and pass it over the 2nd stitch (now, there is 1 stitch on the right needle); *slip 1 purlwise from the left needle to the right one, insert the left needle from left to right through the 1st stitch on the right needle and pass it over the 2nd stitch (now, there is 1 stitch on the right needle)* repeat from * to * until the end of the row.

Note: For trimming, bind off loosely using larger needles than the working ones, in order to create a larger chain of edge stitches, as this type of binding off creates a tight chain of small edge stitches that look already finished.

Pattern 30

Cast on a multiple of 11, plus 2 for symmetry, and plus 2 edge stitches. Eleven-stitch repeat. Repeat rows: 1-4. The edge stitches are not included in the description below and must be added. Slip the first edge stitch; purl the last edge stitch.

Knit through the back leg, purl as follows: with the working yarn in front of the stitch, insert the right needle through the stitch from back to front, move the working yarn under the right needle and pull it through the stitch. The purl stitch that is worked this way sets up the knit stitch to be knitted through the back leg.

Description:

Row 1: *Purl 2, slip 3 onto a cable needle behind your work, knit the next 3, then knit the slipped 3, knit the next 3* repeat from * to * until the end of the row before the edge stitch, purl 2.

Row 2: *Knit 2, purl 9* repeat from * to * until the end of the row before the edge stitch, knit 2.

Row 3: *Purl 2, knit 3, slip the next 3 onto a cable needle in front of your work, knit the next 3, then knit the slipped 3* repeat from * to * until the end of the row before the edge stitch, purl 2.

Row 4: *Knit 2, purl 9* repeat from * to * until the end of the row before the edge stitch, knit 2.

Repeat rows: 1-4.

Bind off as follows: After the last row 3, turn your work over; the Back Side: slip all the stitches from the left needle to the right one; now the working yarn is at the end of the row; turn your work over; the Front Side: slip 2 purlwise from the left needle to the right one, insert the left needle from left to right through the 1st slipped stitch and pass it over the 2nd stitch (now, there is 1 stitch on the right needle); *slip 1 purlwise from the left needle to the right one, insert the left needle from left to right through the 1st stitch on the right needle and pass it over the 2nd stitch (now, there is 1 stitch on the right needle)* repeat from * to * until the end of the row.

Note: For trimming, bind off loosely using larger needles than the working ones, in order to create a larger chain of edge stitches, as this type of binding off creates a tight chain of small edge stitches that look already finished.

Pattern 31

Cast on a multiple of 12, plus 2 for symmetry, and plus 2 edge stitches. Twelve-stitch repeat. Repeat rows: 1-4. The edge stitches are not included in the description below and must be added. Slip the first stitch; purl the last edge stitch.

Knit through the back leg; purl as follows: with the working yarn in front of the stitch, insert the right needle through the stitch from back to front, move the working yarn under the right needle and pull it with the needle through the stitch. The purl stitch that is worked this way sets up the knit stitch to be knitted through the back leg.

Description:

Row 1: *Purl 2, knit 3, slip 3 onto a cable needle behind your work, knit 4, then knit the slipped 3* repeat from * to * until the end of the row before the edge stitch, purl 2.

Row 2: *Knit 2, purl 10* repeat from * to * until the end of the row before the edge stitch, knit 2.

Row 3: *Purl 2, slip 4 onto a cable needle in front of your work, knit 3, then knit the slipped 4, knit the next 3* repeat from * to * until the end of the row before the edge stitch, purl 2.

Row 4: *Knit 2, purl 10* repeat from * to * until the end of the row before the edge stitch, knit 2.

Repeat rows: 1-4.

Bind off as follows: After the last row 3, turn your work over; the Back Side: slip all the stitches from the left needle to the right one; now the working yarn is at the end of the row; turn your work over; the Front Side: slip 2 purlwise from the left needle to the right one, insert the left needle from left to right through the 1st slipped stitch and pass it over the 2nd stitch (now, there is 1 stitch on the right needle); *slip 1 purlwise from the left needle to the right one, insert the left needle from left to right through the 1st stitch on the right needle and pass it over the 2nd stitch (now, there is 1 stitch on the right needle)* repeat from * to * until the end of the row.

Note: For trimming, bind off loosely using larger needles than the working ones, in order to create a larger chain of edge stitches, as this type of binding off creates a tight chain of small edge stitches that look already finished.

Pattern 32

Cast on a multiple of 9, plus 2 edge stitches. Nine-stitch repeat. Repeat rows: 1-8.
The edge stitches are not included in the description below and must be added. Slip the first edge stitch; purl the last edge stitch.

Knit through the back leg; purl as follows: with the working yarn in front of the stitch, insert the right needle through the stitch from back to front, move the working yarn under the right needle and pull it with the needle through the stitch. The purl stitch that is worked this way sets up the knit stitch to be knitted through the back leg. Knit tightly.

Description:

Row 1: *Slip 3 onto a cable needle in front of your work, knit the next 3, then knit the slipped 3, knit the next 3* repeat from * to * until the end of the row.

Row 2: Purl all the stitches.

Row 3: Knit all the stitches.

Row 4: Purl all the stitches.

Row 5: *Knit 3, slip the next 3 onto a cable needle behind your work, knit the next 3, then knit the slipped 3* repeat from * to * until the end of the row.

Row 6: Purl all the stitches.

Row 7: Knit all the stitches.

Row 8: Purl all the stitches.

Repeat rows: 1-8.

Bind off as follows: After the last row 5, turn your work over; the Back Side: slip all the stitches from the left needle to the right one; now the working yarn is at the end of the row; turn your work over; the Front Side: slip 2 purlwise from the left needle to the right one, insert the left needle from left to right through the 1st slipped stitch and pass it over the 2nd stitch (now, there is 1 stitch on the right needle); *slip 1 purlwise from the left needle to the right one, insert the left needle from left to right through the 1st stitch on the right needle and pass it over the 2nd stitch (now, there is 1 stitch on the right needle)* repeat from * to * until the end of the row.

Note: For trimming, bind off loosely using larger needles than the working ones, in order to create a larger chain of edge stitches, as this type of binding off creates a tight chain of small edge stitches that look already finished.

Pattern 33

Cast on a multiple of 10, plus 1 for symmetry, and plus 2 edge stitches. Ten-stitch repeat. Repeat rows: 1-2. The edge stitches are not included in the description below and must be added. Slip the first edge stitch; purl the last edge stitch.

Knit through the back leg; purl as follows: with the working yarn in front of the stitch, insert the right needle through the stitch from back to front, move the working yarn under the right needle and pull it with the needle through the stitch. The purl stitch that is worked this way sets up the knit stitch to be knitted through the back leg. Knit tightly.

Description:

Row 1: *Purl 1, slip 2 onto a cable needle behind your work, knit the next 2, knit the slipped 2, purl 1, slip the next 2 onto a cable needle in front of your work, knit the next 2, knit the slipped 2* repeat from * to * until the end of the row before the edge stitch, purl 1.

Row 2: *Knit 1, purl 4, knit 1, purl 4* repeat from * to * until the end of the row before the edge stitch, knit 1.

Repeat rows: 1-2.

Bind off as follows: After the last row 1, turn your work over; the Back Side: slip all the stitches from the left needle to the right one; now the working yarn is at the end of the row; turn your work over; the Front Side: slip 2 purlwise from the left needle to the right one, insert the left needle from left to right through the 1st slipped stitch and pass it over the 2nd stitch (now, there is 1 stitch on the right needle); *slip 1 purlwise from the left needle to the right one, insert the left needle from left to right through the 1st stitch on the right needle and pass it over the 2nd stitch (now, there is 1 stitch on the right needle)* repeat from * to * until the end of the row.

Note: For trimming, bind off loosely using larger needles than the working ones, in order to create a larger chain of edge stitches, as this type of binding off creates a tight chain of small edge stitches that look already finished.

Pattern 34

Cast on a multiple of 12, plus 2 edge stitches. Twelve-stitch repeat. Repeat rows: 1-8. The edge stitches are not included in the description below and must be added. Slip the first edge stitch; purl the last edge stitch.

Knit through the back leg, purl as follows: with the working yarn in front of the stitch, insert the right needle through the stitch from back to front, move the working yarn under the right needle and pull it with the needle through the stitch. The purl stitch that is worked this way sets up the knit stitch to be knitted through the back leg. Knit tightly.

Description:

Row 1: *Slip 4 onto a cable needle in front of your work, knit the next 4, knit the slipped 4, knit the next 4* repeat from * to * until the end of the row.

Row 2: Purl all the stitches.

Row 3: Knit all the stitches.

Row 4: Purl all the stitches.

Row 5: *Knit 4, slip the next 4 onto a cable needle behind your work, knit the next 4, knit the slipped 4* repeat from * to * until the end of the row.

Row 6: Purl all the stitches.

Row 7: Knit all the stitches.

Row 8: Purl all the stitches.

Repeat rows: 1-8.

Bind off as follows: After the last row 5, turn your work over; the Back Side: slip all the stitches from the left needle to the right one; now the working yarn is at the end of the row; turn your work over; the Front Side: slip 2 purlwise from the left needle to the right one, insert the left needle from left to right through the 1st slipped stitch and pass it over the 2nd stitch (now, there is 1 stitch on the right needle); *slip 1 purlwise from the left needle to the right one, insert the left needle from left to right through the 1st stitch on the right needle and pass it over the 2nd stitch (now, there is 1 stitch on the right needle)* repeat from * to * until the end of the row.

Note: For trimming, bind off loosely using larger needles than the working ones, in order to create a larger chain of edge stitches, as this type of binding off creates a tight chain of small edge stitches that look already finished.

Pattern 35

Cast on a multiple of 12, plus 2 edge stitches. Twelve-stitch repeat. Repeat rows: 1-8. The edge stitches are not included in the description below and must be added. Slip the first edge stitch; purl the last edge stitch.

Knit through the back leg, purl as follows: with the working yarn in front of the stitch, insert the right needle through the stitch from back to front, move the working yarn under the right needle and pull it with the needle through the stitch. The purl stitch that is worked this way sets up the knit stitch to be knitted through the back leg.

Description:

Row 1: *Slip 4 onto a cable needle behind your work, knit the next 4, knit the slipped 4, knit the next 4* repeat from * to * until the end of the row.

Row 2: Purl all the stitches.

Row 3: Knit all the stitches.

Row 4: Purl all the stitches.

Row 5: *Knit 4, slip the next 4 onto a cable needle in front of your work, knit the next 4, knit the slipped 4* repeat from * to * until the end of the row.

Row 6: Purl all the stitches.

Row 7: knit all the stitches.

Row 8: purl all the stitches.

Repeat rows: 1-8.

Bind off as follows: After the last row 5, turn your work over; the Back Side: slip all the stitches from the left needle to the right one, now the working yarn is at the end of the row; turn your work over; the Front Side: slip 2 purlwise from the left needle to the right one, insert the left needle from left to right through the 1st slipped stitch and pass it over the 2nd stitch (now, there is 1 stitch on the right needle); *slip 1 purlwise from the left needle to the right one, insert the left needle from left to right through the 1st stitch on the right needle and pass it over the 2nd stitch (now, there is 1 stitch on the right needle)* repeat from * to * until the end of the row.

Note: For trimming, bind off loosely using larger needles than the working ones, in order to create a larger chain of edge stitches, as this type of binding off creates a tight chain of small edge stitches that look already finished.

Pattern 36

Cast on a multiple of 18, plus 2 edge stitches. Eighteen-stitch repeat. Repeat rows: 1-12. The edge stitches are not included in the description below and must be added. Slip the first edge stitch; purl the last edge stitch.

Knit through the back leg; purl as follows: with the working yarn in front of the stitch, insert the right needle through the stitch from back to front, move the working yarn under the right needle and pull it with the needle through the stitch. The purl stitch that is worked this way sets up the knit stitch to be knitted through the back leg.

Description:

Row 1: *Slip 6 onto a cable needle in front of your work, knit the next 6, then knit the slipped 6, knit the next 6* repeat from * to * until the end of the row.

Row 2: Purl all the stitches.

Row 3: Knit all the stitches.

Row 4: Purl all the stitches.

Row 5: Knit all the stitches.

Row 6: Purl all the stitches.

Row 7: *Knit 6, slip the next 6 onto a cable needle behind your work, knit the next 6, then knit the slipped 6* repeat from * to * until the end of the row.

Row 8: Purl all the stitches.

Row 9: Knit all the stitches.

Row 10: Purl all the stitches.

Row 11: Knit all the stitches.

Row 12: Purl all the stitches.

Repeat rows: 1-12.

Bind off as follows: After the last row 7, turn your work over; the Back Side: slip all the stitches from the left needle to the right one, now the working yarn is at the end of the row; turn your work over; the Front Side: slip 2 purlwise from the left needle to the right one, insert the left needle from left to right through the 1st slipped stitch and pass it over the 2nd stitch (now, there is 1 stitch on the right needle); *slip 1 purlwise from the left needle to

the right one, insert the left needle from left to right through the 1st stitch on the right needle and pass it over the 2nd stitch (now, there is 1 stitch on the right needle)* repeat from * to * until the end of the row.

Note: For trimming, bind off loosely using larger needles than the working ones, in order to create a larger chain of edge stitches, as this type of binding off creates a tight chain of small edge stitches that look already finished.

Pattern 37

Cast on a multiple of 12, plus 2 edge stitches. Twelve-stitch repeat. Repeat rows: 1-16. The edge stitches are not included in the description below and must be added. Slip the first edge stitch; purl the last edge stitch.

Knit through the back leg; purl as follows: with the working yarn in front of the stitch, insert the right needle through the stitch from back to front, move the working yarn under the right needle and pull it with the needle through the stitch. The purl stitch that is worked this way sets up the knit stitch to be knitted through the back leg. Knit tightly.

Description:

Row 1: *Knit 6, slip the next 3 onto a cable needle in front of your work, knit the next 3, knit the slipped 3* repeat from * to * until the end of the row.

Row 2: Purl all the stitches.

Row 3: Knit all the stitches.

Row 4: Purl all the stitches.

Row 5: Knit all the stitches.

Row 6: Purl all the stitches.

Row 7: Knit all the stitches.

Row 8: Purl all the stitches.

Row 9: *Slip 3 onto a cable needle behind your work, knit the next 3, knit the slipped 3, knit the next 6* repeat from * to * until the end of the row.

Row 10: Purl all the stitches.

Row 11: Knit all the stitches.

Row 12: Purl all the stitches.

Row 13: Knit all the stitches.

Row 14: Purl all the stitches.

Row 15: Knit all the stitches.

Row 16: Purl all the stitches.

Repeat rows: 1-16.

Bind off as follows: After the last row 9, turn your work over; the Back Side: slip all the stitches from the left needle to the right one, now the working yarn is at the end of the row; turn your work over; the Front Side: slip 2 purlwise from the left needle to the right one, insert the left needle from left to right through the 1st slipped stitch and pass it over the 2nd stitch (now, there is 1 stitch on the right needle); *slip 1 purlwise from the left needle to the right one, insert the left needle from left to right through the 1st stitch on the right needle and pass it over the 2nd stitch (now, there is 1 stitch on the right needle)* repeat from * to * until the end of the row.

Note: For trimming, bind off loosely using larger needles than the working ones, in order to create a larger chain of edge stitches, as this type of binding off creates a tight chain of small edge stitches that look already finished.

Pattern 38

Cast on a multiple of 27, plus 3 for symmetry, and plus 2 edge stitches. Twenty-seven-stitch repeat. Repeat rows: 1-4. The edge stitches are not included in the description below and must be added. Slip the first edge stitch; purl the last edge stitch as if to purl in knitting through the back leg as follows: insert the right needle through the stitch from back to front, move the working yarn under the right needle and pull it with the needle through the stitch.

Knit through the front leg, purl as follows: with the working yarn in front of your work, insert the right needle from back to front through the stitch and wrap the working yarn counterclockwise around the tip of the right needle, then pull the working yarn with the right needle through the stitch. The purl stitch that is worked this way sets up the knit stitch to be knitted through the front leg.

Description:

Row 1: *purl 3, knit 4, slip the next 4 onto a cable needle behind your work, knit the next 4, then knit the slipped 4, slip the next 4 onto a cable needle in front of your work, knit the next 4, then knit the slipped 4, knit the next 4* repeat from * to * until the end of the row before the edge stitch, purl 3.

Row 2: *knit 3, purl 24* repeat from * to * until the end of the row before the edge stitch, knit 3.

Row 3: *purl 3, slip 4 onto a cable needle behind your work, knit the next 4, then knit the slipped 4, knit the next 8, slip the next 4 onto a cable needle in front of your work, knit the next 4, then knit the slipped 4* repeat from * to * until the end of the row before the edge stitch, purl 3.

Row 4: *knit 3, purl 24* repeat from * to * until the end of the row before the edge stitch, knit 3.

Repeat rows: 1-4.

Bind off as follows: After the last row 3, turn your work over; the Back Side: slip all the stitches from the left needle to the right one, now the working yarn is at the end of the row; turn your work over; the Front Side: slip 2 purlwise from the left needle to the right one, insert the left needle from left to right through the 1st slipped stitch and pass it over the 2nd stitch (now, there is 1 stitch on the right needle); *slip 1 purlwise from the left needle to the right one, insert the left needle from left to right through the 1st stitch on the right needle and pass it over the 2nd stitch (now, there is 1 stitch on the right needle)* repeat from * to * until the end of the row.

Note: For trimming, bind off loosely using larger needles than the working ones, in order to create a larger chain of edge stitches, as this type of binding off creates a tight chain of small edge stitches that look already finished.

Pattern 39

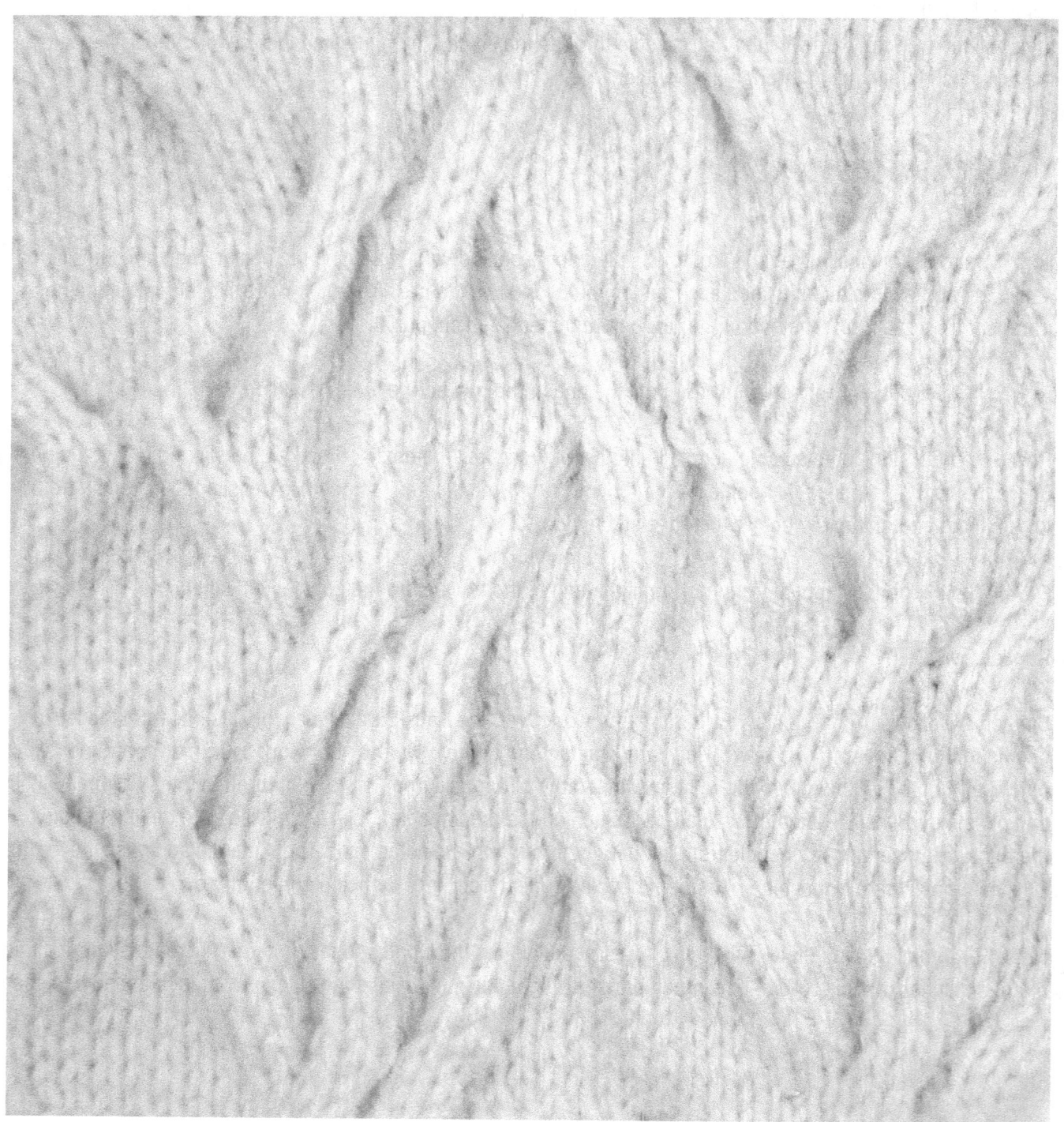

Cast on a multiple of 24, plus 2 edge stitches. Twenty-four-stitch repeat. Repeat rows: 1-16. The edge stitches are not included in the description below and must be added. Slip the first edge stitch; purl the last edge stitch.

Knit through the back leg; purl as follows: with the working yarn in front of the stitch, insert the right needle through the stitch from back to front, move the working yarn under the right needle and pull it with the needle through the stitch. The purl stitch that is worked this way sets up the knit stitch to be knitted through the back leg. Knit tightly.

Description:

Row 1: *Slip 3 onto a cable needle behind your work, knit the next 3, knit the slipped 3, slip the next 3 onto a cable needle behind your work, knit the next 3, knit the slipped 3, knit the next 12* repeat from * to * until the end of the row.

Row 2: Purl all the stitches.

Row 3: Knit all the stitches.

Row 4: Purl all the stitches.

Row 5: Knit all the stitches.

Row 6: Purl all the stitches.

Row 7: Knit all the stitches.

Row 8: Purl all the stitches.

Row 9: *Knit 12, slip the next 3 onto a cable needle in front of your work, knit the next 3, knit the slipped 3, slip the next 3 onto a cable needle in front of your work, knit the next 3, knit the slipped 3* repeat from * to * until the end of the row.

Row 10: Purl all the stitches.

Row 11: Knit all the stitches.

Row 12: Purl all the stitches.

Row 13: Knit all the stitches.

Row 14: Purl all the stitches.

Row 15: Knit all the stitches.

Row 16: Purl all the stitches.

Repeat rows: 1-16.

Bind off as follows: After the last row 3, turn your work over; the Back Side: slip all the stitches from the left needle to the right one; now the working yarn is at the end of the row; turn your work over; the Front Side: slip 2 purlwise from the left needle to the right one, insert the left needle from left to right through the 1st slipped stitch and pass it over the 2nd stitch (now, there is 1 stitch on the right needle); *slip 1 purlwise from the left needle to the right one, insert the left needle from left to right through the 1st stitch on the right needle and pass it over the 2nd stitch (now, there is 1 stitch on the right needle)* repeat from * to * until the end of the row.

Note: For trimming, bind off loosely using larger needles than the working ones, in order to create a larger chain of edge stitches, as this type of binding off creates a tight chain of small edge stitches that look already finished.

Pattern 40

Cast on a multiple of 12, plus 2 edge stitches. Twelve-stitch repeat. Repeat rows: 1-8. The edge stitches are not included in the description below and must be added. Slip the first edge stitch; purl the last edge stitch.

Knit through the back leg, purl as follows: with the working yarn in front of the stitch, insert the right needle through the stitch from back to front, move the working yarn under the right needle and pull it with the needle through the stitch. The purl stitch that is worked this way sets up the knit stitch to be knitted through the back leg.

Description:

Row 1: *Knit 6, slip the next 3 onto a cable needle in front of your work, knit the next 3, then knit the slipped 3* repeat from * to * until the end of the row.

Row 2: Purl all the stitches.

Row 3: Knit all the stitches.

Row 4: Purl all the stitches.

Row 5: *Slip 3 onto a cable needle behind your work, knit the next 3, then knit the slipped 3, knit the next 6* repeat from * to * until the end of the row.

Row 6: Purl all the stitches.

Row 7: Knit all the stitches.

Row 8: Purl all the stitches.

Repeat rows: 1-8.

Bind off as follows: After the last row 1, turn your work over; the Back Side: slip all the stitches from the left needle to the right one; now the working yarn is at the end of the row; turn your work over; the Front Side: slip 2 purlwise from the left needle to the right one, insert the left needle from left to right through the 1st slipped stitch and pass it over the 2nd stitch (now, there is 1 stitch on the right needle); *slip 1 purlwise from the left needle to the right one, insert the left needle from left to right through the 1st stitch on the right needle and pass it over the 2nd stitch (now, there is 1 stitch on the right needle)* repeat from * to * until the end of the row.

Note: For trimming, bind off loosely using larger needles than the working ones, in order to create a larger chain of edge stitches, as this type of binding off creates a tight chain of small edge stitches that look already finished.

Pattern 41

Cast on a multiple of 12, plus 2 edge stitches. Twelve-stitch repeat. Repeat rows: 1-8.
The edge stitches are not included in the description below and must be added. Slip the first edge stitch; purl the last edge stitch.

Knit through the back leg, purl as follows: with the working yarn in front of the stitch, insert the right needle through the stitch from back to front, move the working yarn under the right needle and pull it through the stitch. The purl stitch that is worked this way sets up the knit stitch to be knitted through the back leg.

Description:

Row 1: *Knit 6, slip the next 3 onto a cable needle behind your work, knit the next 3, knit the slipped 3* repeat from * to * until the end of the row.

Row 2: Purl all the stitches.

Row 3: Knit all the stitches.

Row 4: Purl all the stitches.

Row 5: *Slip 3 onto a cable needle behind your work, knit the next 3, knit the slipped 3, knit the next 6* repeat from * to * until the end of the row.

Row 6: Purl all the stitches.

Row 7: Knit all the stitches.

Row 8: Purl all the stitches.

Repeat rows: 1-8.

Bind off as follows: After the last row 5, turn your work over; the Back Side: slip all the stitches from the left needle to the right one; now the working yarn is at the end of the row; turn your work over; the Front Side: slip 2 purlwise from the left needle to the right one, insert the left needle from left to right through the 1st slipped stitch and pass it over the 2nd stitch (now, there is 1 stitch on the right needle); *slip 1 purlwise from the left needle to the right one, insert the left needle from left to right through the 1st stitch on the right needle and pass it over the 2nd stitch (now, there is 1 stitch on the right needle)* repeat from * to * until the end of the row.

Note: For trimming, bind off loosely using larger needles than the working ones, in order to create a larger chain of edge stitches, as this type of binding off creates a tight chain of small edge stitches that look already finished.

Pattern 42

Cast on a multiple of 15, plus 3 for symmetry, and plus 2 edge stitches. Fifteen-stitch repeat. Repeat rows: 1-8. The edge stitches are not included in the description below and must be added. Slip the first edge stitch; purl the last edge stitch.

Knit through the back leg, purl as follows: with the working yarn in front of the stitch, insert the right needle through the stitch from back to front, move the working yarn under the right needle and pull it through the stitch. The purl stitch that is worked this way sets up the knit stitch to be knitted through the back leg.

Description:

Row 1: *Purl 3, slip 3 onto a cable needle in front of your work, knit the next 3, knit the slipped 3, knit then next 6* repeat from * to * until the end of the row before the edge stitch, purl 3.

Row 2: *Knit 3, purl 12* repeat from * to * until the end of the row before the edge stitch, knit 3.

Row 3: *Purl 3, knit 12* repeat from * to * until the end of the row before the edge stitch, purl 3.

Row 4: *Knit 3, purl 12* repeat from * to * until the end of the row before the edge stitch, knit 3.

Row 5: *Purl 3, knit 6, slip the next 3 onto a cable needle behind your work, knit the next 3, knit the slipped 3* repeat from * to * until the end of the row before the edge stitch, purl 3.

Row 6: *Knit 3, purl 12* repeat from * to * until the end of the row before the edge stitch, knit 3.

Row 7: *Purl 3, knit 12* repeat from * to * until the end of the row before the edge stitch, purl 3.

Row 8: *Knit 3, purl 12* repeat from * to * until the end of the row before the edge stitch, knit 3.

Repeat rows: 1-8.

Bind off as follows: After the last row 5, turn your work over; the Back Side: slip all the stitches from the left needle to the right one; now the working yarn is at the end of the row; turn your work over; the Front Side: slip 2 purlwise from the left needle to the right one, insert the left needle from left to right through the 1st slipped stitch and pass it over the 2nd stitch (now, there is 1 stitch on the right needle); *slip 1 purlwise from the left needle to the right one, insert the left needle from left to right through the 1st stitch on the right needle and pass it over the 2nd stitch (now, there is 1 stitch on the right needle)* repeat from * to * until the end of the row.

Note: For trimming, bind off loosely using larger needles than the working ones, in order to create a larger chain of edge stitches, as this type of binding off creates a tight chain of small edge stitches that look already finished.

Pattern 43

Cast on a multiple of 21, plus 3 for symmetry, and plus 2 edge stitches. Twenty-one-stitch repeat. Repeat rows: 1-4. The edge stitches are not included in the description below and must be added. Slip the first edge stitch; purl the last edge stitch as if to purl in knitting through the back leg as follows: with the working yarn in front of the stitch, insert the right needle through the stitch from back to front, move the working yarn under the right needle and pull it through the stitch.

Knit through the front leg, purl as follows: with the working yarn in front of your work, insert the right needle through the stitch from back to front and wrap the working yarn counterclockwise around the tip of the right needle, then pull the working yarn with the right needle through the stitch. The purl stitch that is worked this way sets up the knit stitch to be knitted through the front leg.

Description:

Row 1: *purl 3, knit 3, slip the next 3 onto a cable needle behind your work, knit the next 3, then knit the slipped 3, slip the next 3 onto a cable needle in front of your work, knit the next 3, then knit the slipped 3, knit the next 3* repeat from * to * until the end of the row before the edge stitch, purl 3.

Row 2: *knit 3, purl 18* repeat from * to * until the end of the row before the edge stitch, knit 3.

Row 3: *purl 3, slip 3 onto a cable needle behind your work, knit the next 3, then knit the slipped 3, knit the next 6, slip the next 3 onto a cable needle in front of your work, knit the next 3, then knit the slipped 3* repeat from * to * until the end of the row before the edge stitch, purl 3.

Row 4: *knit 3, purl 18* repeat from * to * until the end of the row before the edge stitch, knit 3.

Repeat rows: 1-4.

Bind off as follows: After the last row 3, turn your work over; the Back Side: slip all the stitches from the left needle to the right one; now the working yarn is at the end of the row; turn your work over; the Front Side: slip 2 purlwise from the left needle to the right one, insert the left needle from left to right through the 1st slipped stitch and pass it over the 2nd stitch (now, there is 1 stitch on the right needle); *slip 1 purlwise from the left needle to the right one, insert the left needle from left to right through the 1st stitch on the right needle and pass it over the 2nd stitch (now, there is 1 stitch on the right needle)* repeat from * to * until the end of the row.

Note: For trimming, bind off loosely using larger needles than the working ones, in order to create a larger chain of edge stitches, as this type of binding off creates a tight chain of small edge stitches that look already finished.

Pattern 44

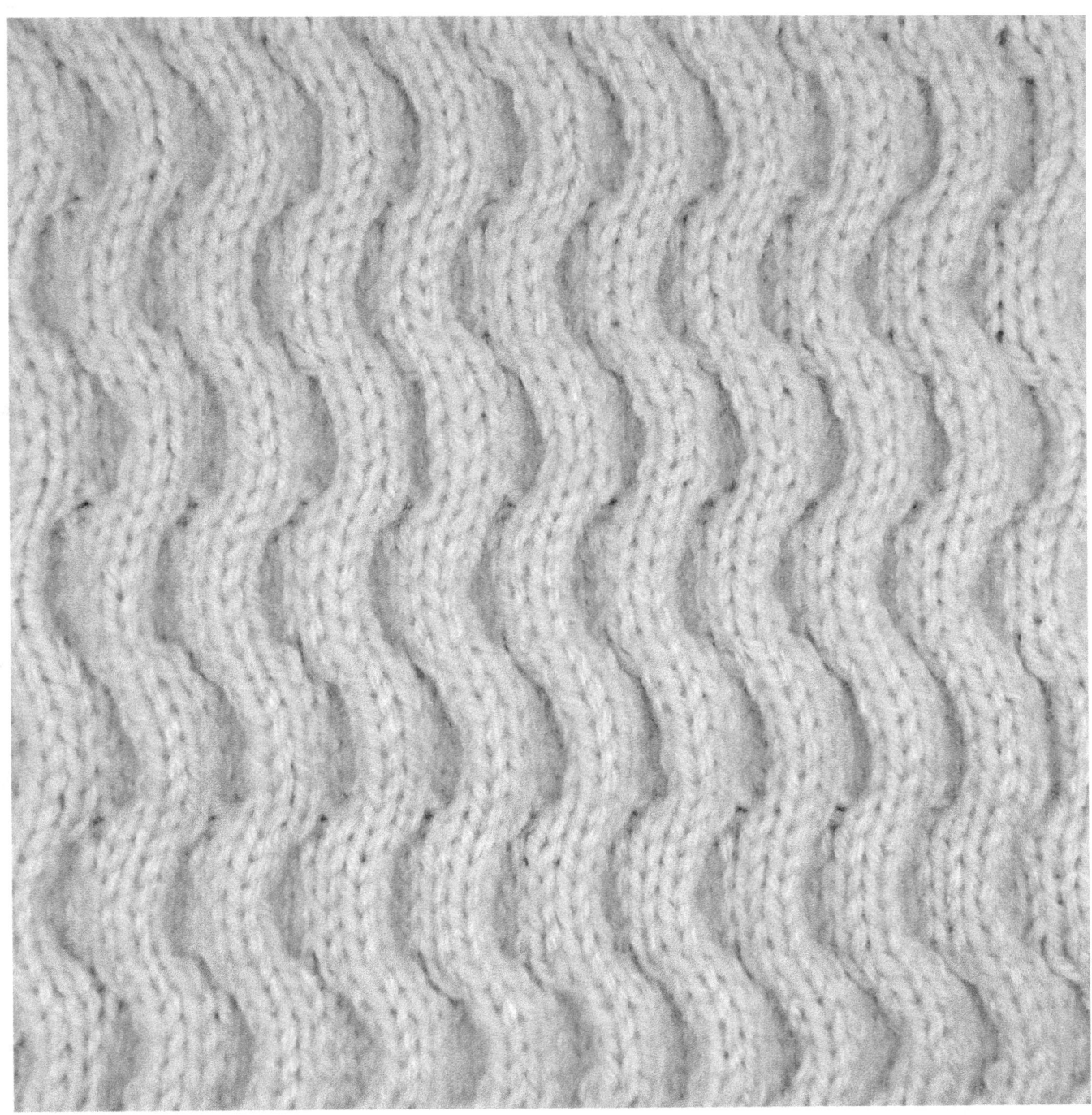

Cast on a multiple of 6, plus 2 edge stitches. Six-stitch repeat. Repeat rows: 1-12.
The edge stitches are not included in the description below and must be added. Slip the first edge stitch; purl the last edge stitch.

Knit through the back leg, purl as follows: with the working yarn in front of the stitch, insert the right needle through the stitch from back to front, move the working yarn under the right needle and pull it with the needle through the stitch. The purl stitch that is worked this way sets up the knit stitch to be knitted through the back leg.

Description:

Row 1: *Slip 3 onto a cable needle behind your work, knit the next 3, knit the slipped 3* repeat from * to * until the end of the row.

Row 2: Purl all the stitches.

Row 3: Knit all the stitches.

Row 4: Purl all the stitches.

Row 5: Knit all the stitches.

Row 6: Purl all the stitches.

Row 7: *Slip 3 onto a cable needle in front of your work, knit the next 3, knit the slipped 3* repeat from * to * until the end of the row.

Row 8: Purl all the stitches.

Row 9: Knit all the stitches.

Row 10: Purl all the stitches.

Row 11: Knit all the stitches.

Row 12: Purl all the stitches.

Repeat rows: 1-12.

Bind off as follows: After the last row 7, turn your work over; the Back Side: slip all the stitches from the left needle to the right one; now the working yarn is at the end of the row; turn your work over; the Front Side: slip 2 purlwise from the left needle to the right one, insert the left needle from left to right through the 1st slipped stitch and pass it over the 2nd stitch (now, there is 1 stitch on the right needle); *slip 1 purlwise from the left needle to

the right one, insert the left needle from left to right through the 1st stitch on the right needle and pass it over the 2nd stitch (now, there is 1 stitch on the right needle)* repeat from * to * until the end of the row.

Note: For trimming, bind off loosely using larger needles than the working ones, in order to create a larger chain of edge stitches, as this type of binding off creates a tight chain of small edge stitches that look already finished.

Pattern 45

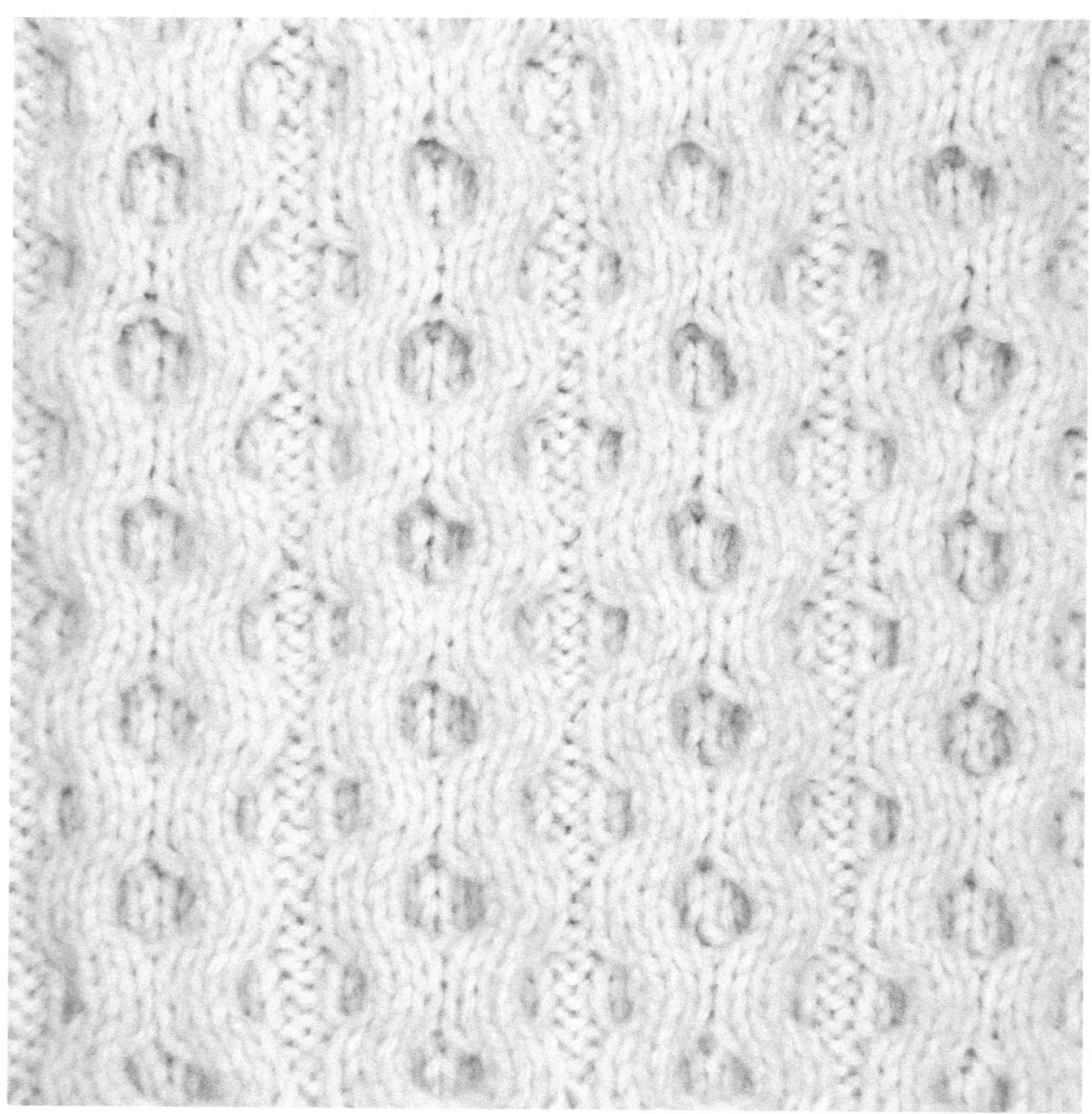

Cast on a multiple of 14, plus 2 for symmetry, and plus 2 edge stitches. Fourteen-stitch repeat. Repeat rows: 1-8. The edge stitches are not included in the description below and must be added. Slip the first edge stitch, purl the last edge stitch.

Knit through the back leg, purl as follows: with the working yarn in front of the stitch, insert the right needle through the stitch from back to front, move the working yarn under the right needle and pull it with the needle through the stitch. The purl stitch that is worked this way sets up the knit stitch to be knitted through the back leg. Knit tightly.

Description:

Row 1: *Purl 2, slip 3 onto a cable needle behind your work, knit the next 3, then knit the slipped 3, slip the next 3 onto a cable needle in front of your work, knit the next 3, then knit the slipped 3* repeat from * to * until the end of the row before the edge stitch, purl 2.

Row 2: *Knit 2, purl 12* repeat from * to * until the end of the row before the edge stitch, knit 2.

Row 3: *Purl 2, knit 12* repeat from * to * until the end of the row before the edge stitch, purl 2.

Row 4: *Knit 2, purl 12* repeat from * to * until the end of the row before the edge stitch, knit 2.

Row 5: *Purl 2, slip 3 onto a cable needle in front of your work, knit the next 3, then knit the slipped 3 as follows: knit 2 through the back legs, knit 1 through the front leg, slip the next 3 onto a cable needle behind your work, knit the next 3, then knit the slipped 3* repeat from * to * until the end of the row before the edge stitch, purl 2.

Row 6: *Knit 2, purl 12* repeat from * to * until the end of the row before the edge stitch, knit 2.

Row 7: *Purl 2, knit 12* repeat from * to * until the end of the row before the edge stitch, purl 2.

Row 8: *Knit 2, purl 12* repeat from * to * until the end of the row before the edge stitch, knit 2.

Repeat rows: 1-8.

Bind off as follows: After the last row 5, turn your work over; the Back Side: slip all the stitches from the left needle to the right one; now the working yarn is at the end of the row; turn your work over; the Front Side: slip 2 purlwise from the left needle to the right one, insert the left needle from left to right through the 1st slipped stitch and pass it over the 2nd stitch (now, there is 1 stitch on the right needle); *slip 1 purlwise from the left needle to the right one, insert the left needle from left to right through the 1st stitch on the right needle and pass it over the 2nd stitch (now, there is 1 stitch on the right needle)* repeat from * to * until the end of the row.

Note: For trimming, bind off loosely using larger needles than the working ones, in order to create a larger chain of edge stitches, as this type of binding off creates a tight chain of small edge stitches that look already finished.

Pattern 46

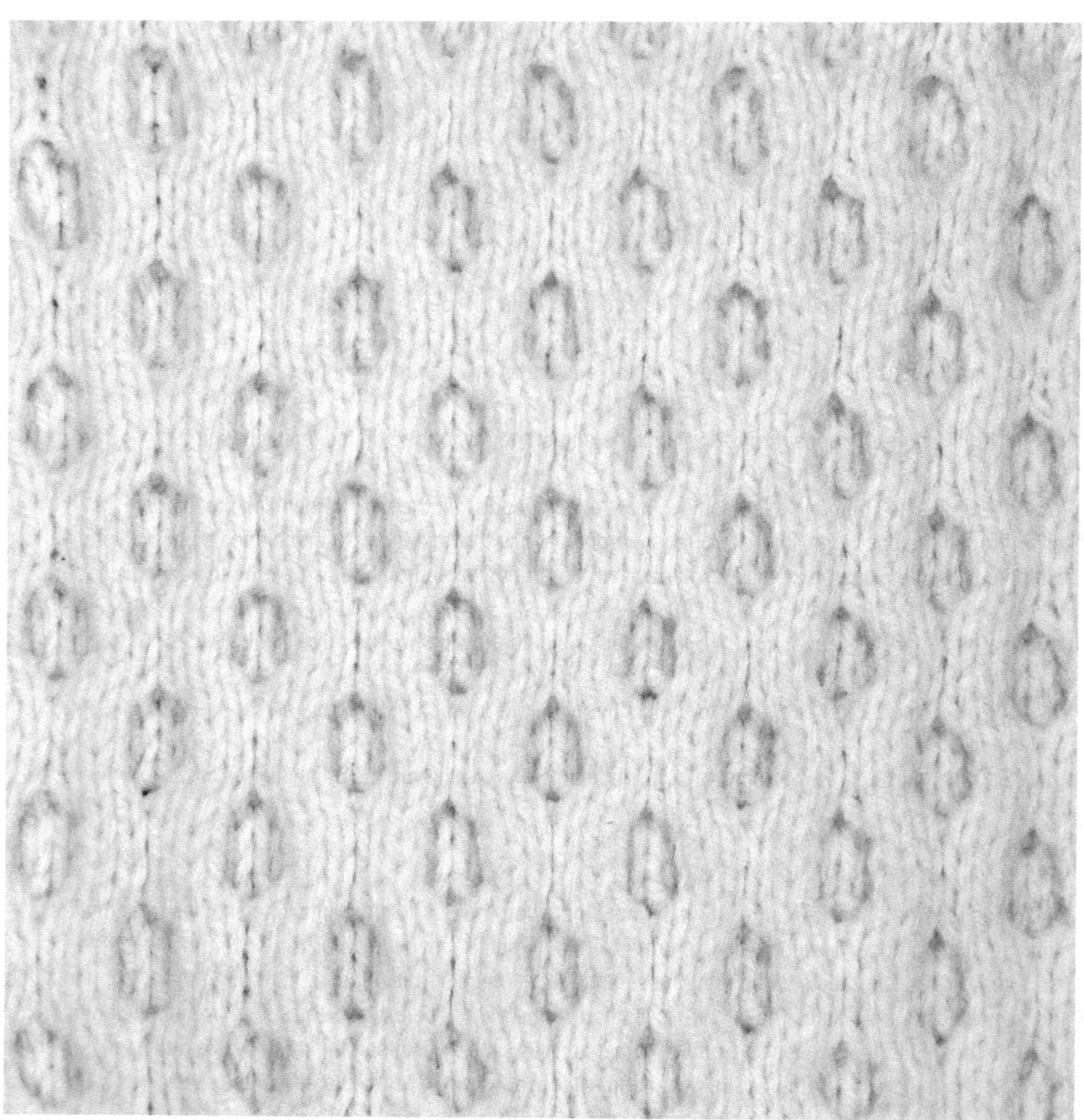

Cast on a multiple of 12, plus 2 edge stitches. Twelve-stitch-repeat. Repeat rows: 1-8. The edge stitches are not included in the description below and must be added. Slip the first edge stitch, purl the last edge stitch.

Knit through the back leg, purl as follows: with the working yarn in front of the stitch, insert the right needle through the stitch from back to front, move the working yarn under the right needle and pull it with the needle through the stitch. The purl stitch that is worked this way sets up the knit stitch to be knitted through the back leg. Knit tightly.

Description:

Row 1: *Slip 3 onto a cable needle behind your work, knit the next 3, then knit the slipped 3, slip the next 3 onto a cable needle in front of your work, knit the next 3, then knit the slipped 3 as follows: knit 2 through the back legs, knit 1 through the front leg* repeat from * to * until the end of the row.

Row 2: Purl all the stitches.

Row 3: Knit all the stitches.

Row 4: Purl all the stitches.

Row 5: *Slip 3 onto a cable needle in front of your work, knit the next 3, then knit the slipped 3 as follows: knit 2 through the back legs, knit 1 through the front leg, then slip the next 3 onto a cable needle behind your work, knit the next 3, then knit the slipped 3* repeat from * to * until the end of the row.

Row 6: Purl all the stitches.

Row 7: Knit all the stitches.

Row 8: Purl all the stitches.

Repeat rows: 1-8.

Bind off as follows: After the last row 5, turn your work over; the Back Side: slip all the stitches from the left needle to the right one; now the working yarn is at the end of the row; turn your work over; the Front Side: slip 2 purlwise from the left needle to the right one, insert the left needle from left to right through the 1st slipped stitch and pass it over the 2nd stitch (now, there is 1 stitch on the right needle); *slip 1 purlwise from the left needle to the right one, insert the left needle from left to right through the 1st stitch on the right needle and pass it over the 2nd stitch (now, there is 1 stitch on the right needle)* repeat from * to * until the end of the row.

Note: For trimming, bind off loosely using larger needles than the working ones, in order to create a larger chain of edge stitches, as this type of binding off creates a tight chain of small edge stitches that look already finished.

Pattern 47

Cast on a multiple of 18, plus 2, and plus 2 edge stitches. Eighteen-stitch repeat. Repeat rows: 1-14. The edge stitches are not included in the description below and must be added. Slip the first edge stitch; purl the last edge stitch.

Knit through the back leg, purl as follows: with the working yarn in front of the stitch, insert the right needle through the stitch from back to front, move the working yarn under the right needle and pull it with the needle through the stitch. The purl stitch that is worked this way sets up the knit stitch to be knitted through the back leg.

Description:

Row 1: *Purl 2, slip 4 onto a cable needle in front of your work, knit the next 4, then knit the slipped 4, knit the next 8* repeat from * to * until the end of the row before the edge stitch, purl 2.

Row 2: *knit 2, purl 16* repeat from * to * until the end of the row before the edge stitch, knit 2.

Row 3: *Purl 2, knit 16* repeat from * to * until the end of the row before the edge stitch, purl 2.

Row 4: *Knit 2, purl 16* repeat from * to * until the end of the row before the edge stitch, knit 2.

Row 5: *Purl 2, knit 16* repeat from * to * until the end of the row before the edge stitch, purl 2.

Row 6: *Knit 2, purl 16* repeat from * to * until the end of the row before the edge stitch, knit 2.

Row 7: *Purl 2, knit 16* repeat from * to * until the end of the row before the edge stitch, purl 2.

Row 8: *Knit 2, purl 16* repeat from * to * until the end of the row before the edge stitch, knit 2.

Row 9: *Purl 2, knit 8, slip 4 onto a cable needle behind your work, knit the next 4, then knit the slipped 4* repeat from * to * until the end of the row before the edge stitch, purl 2.

Row 10: *Knit 2, purl 16* repeat from * to * until the end of the row before the edge stitch, knit 2.

Row 11: *Purl 2, knit 16* repeat from * to * until the end of the row before the edge stitch, purl 2.

Row 12: *Knit 2, purl 16* repeat from * to * until the end of the row before the edge stitch, knit 2.

Row 13: *Purl 2, knit 16* repeat from * to * until the end of the row before the edge stitch, purl 2.

Row 14: *Knit 2, purl 16* repeat from * to * until the end of the row before the edge stitch, knit 2.

Repeat rows: 1-14.

Bind off as follows: After the last row 1, turn your work over; the Back Side: slip all the stitches from the left needle to the right one; now the working yarn is at the end of the row; turn your work over; the Front Side: slip 2 purlwise from the left needle to the right one, insert the left needle from left to right through the 1st slipped stitch and pass it over the 2nd stitch (now, there is 1 stitch on the right needle); *slip 1 purlwise from the left needle to

the right one, insert the left needle from left to right through the 1st stitch on the right needle and pass it over the 2nd stitch (now, there is 1 stitch on the right needle)* repeat from * to * until the end of the row.

Note: For trimming, bind off loosely using larger needles than the working ones, in order to create a larger chain of edge stitches, as this type of binding off creates a tight chain of small edge stitches that look already finished.

Pattern 48

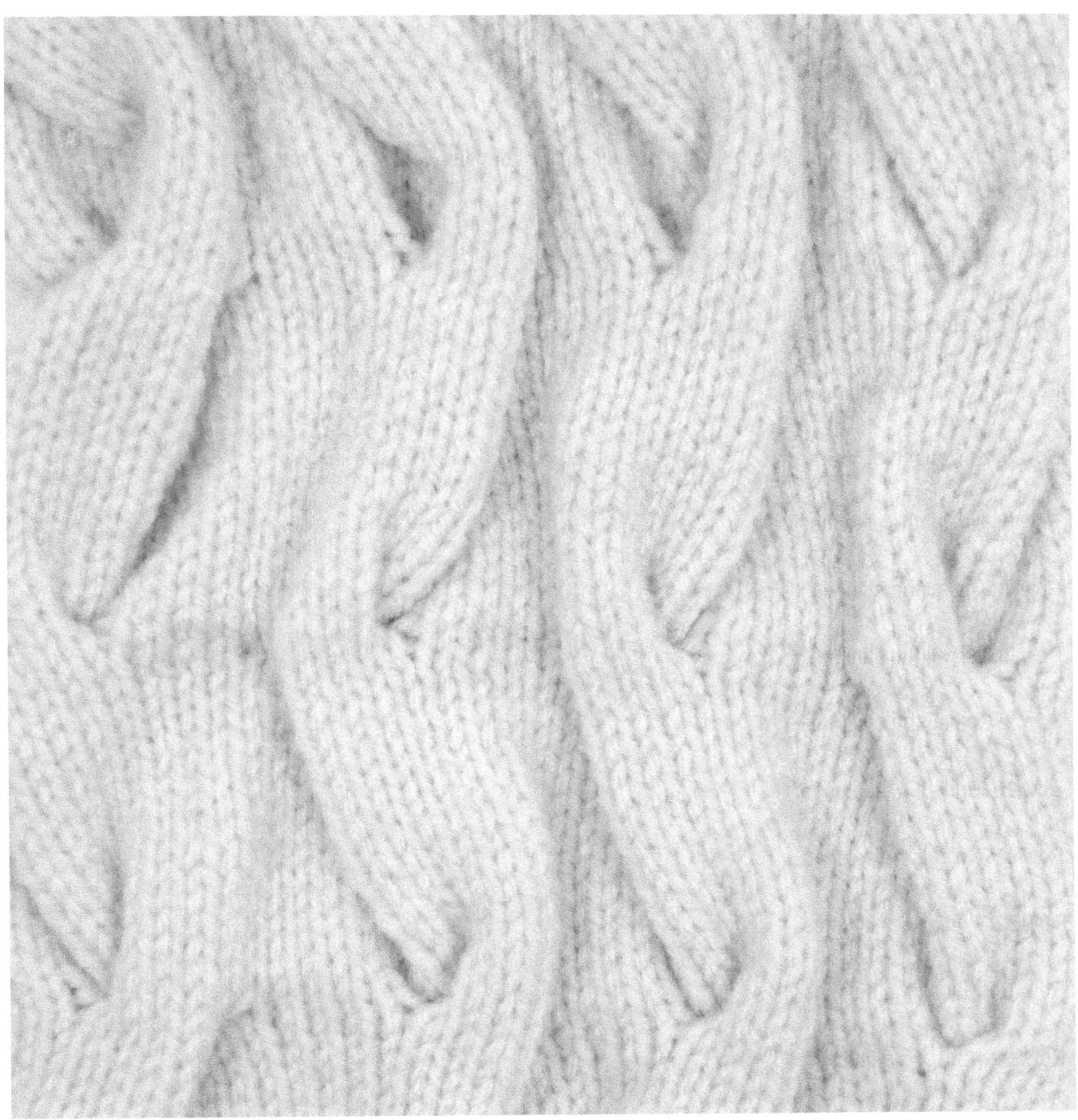

Cast on a multiple of 16, plus 2 edge stitches. Sixteen-stitch repeat. Repeat rows: 1-36. The edge stitches are not included in the description below and must be added. Slip the first edge stitch; purl the last edge stitch.

Knit through the back leg, purl as follows: with the working yarn in front of the stitch, insert the right needle through the stitch from back to front, move the working yarn under the right needle and pull it with the needle through the stitch. The purl stitch that is worked this way sets up the knit stitch to be knitted through the back leg.

Description:

Row 1: *Knit 4, slip the next 6 onto a cable needle in front of your work, knit the next 6, knit the slipped 6* repeat from * to * until the end of the row.

Row 2: Purl all the stitches.

Row 3: Knit all the stitches.

Row 4: Purl all the stitches.

Row 5: Knit all the stitches.

Row 6: Purl all the stitches.

Row 7: Knit all the stitches.

Row 8: Purl all the stitches.

Row 9: Knit all the stitches.

Row 10: Purl all the stitches.

Row 11: Knit all the stitches.

Row 12: Purl all the stitches.

Row 13: Knit all the stitches.

Row 14: Purl all the stitches.

Row 15: Knit all the stitches.

Row 16: Purl all the stitches.

Row 17: Knit all the stitches.

Row 18: Purl all the stitches.

Row 19: *Slip 6 onto a cable needle behind your work, knit the next 6, knit the slipped 6, knit the next 4* repeat from * to * until the end of the row.

Row 20: Purl all the stitches.

Row 21: Knit all the stitches.

Row 22: Purl all the stitches.

Row 23: Knit all the stitches.

Row 24: Purl all the stitches.

Row 25: Knit all the stitches.

Row 26: Purl all the stitches.

Row 27: Knit all the stitches.

Row 28: Purl all the stitches.

Row 29: Knit all the stitches.

Row 30: Purl all the stitches.

Row 31: Knit all the stitches.

Row 32: Purl all the stitches.

Row 33: Knit all the stitches.

Row 34: Purl all the stitches.

Row 35: Knit all the stitches.

Row 36: Purl all the stitches.

Repeat rows: 1-36.

Bind off as follows: After the last row 19, turn your work over; the Back Side: slip all the stitches from the left needle to the right one; now the working yarn is at the end of the row; turn your work over; the Front Side: slip 2 purlwise from the left needle to the right one, insert the left needle from left to right through the 1st slipped stitch and pass it over the 2nd stitch (now, there is 1 stitch on the right needle); *slip 1 purlwise from the left needle to the right one, insert the left needle from left to right through the 1st stitch on the right needle and pass it over the 2nd stitch (now, there is 1 stitch on the right needle)* repeat from * to * until the end of the row.

Note: For trimming, bind off loosely using larger needles than the working ones, in order to create a larger chain of edge stitches, as this type of binding off creates a tight chain of small edge stitches that look already finished.

Pattern 49

Cast on a multiple of 27, plus 3 for symmetry, and plus 2 edge stitches. Twenty-seven-stitch repeat. Repeat rows: 1-8. The edge stitches are not included in the description below and must be added. Slip the first edge stitch; purl the last edge stitch.

Knit through the back leg, purl as follows: with the working yarn in front of the stitch, insert the right needle through the stitch from back to front, then move the working yarn under the right needle and pull it through the stitch. The purl stitch that is worked this way sets up the knit stitch to be knitted through the back leg.

Description:

Row 1: *purl 3, knit 12, slip the next 6 in front of your work, knit the next 6, then knit the slipped 6* repeat from * to * until the end of the row before the edge stitch, purl 3.

Row 2: *knit 3, purl 24 * repeat from * to * until the end of the row before the edge stitch, knit 3.

Row 3: *purl 3, knit 24* repeat from * to * until the end of the row before the edge stitch, purl 3.

Row 4: *knit 3, purl 24* repeat from * to * until the end of the row before the edge stitch, knit 3.

Row 5: *purl 3, slip 6 behind your work, knit the next 6, then knit the slipped 6, knit the next 12* repeat from * to * until the end of the row before the edge stitch, purl 3.

Row 6: *knit 3, purl 24* repeat from * to * until the end of the row before the edge stitch, knit 3.

Row 7: *purl 3, knit 24* repeat from * to * until the end of the row before the edge stitch, purl 3.

Row 8: *knit 3, purl 24* repeat from * to * until the end of the row before the edge stitch, knit 3.

Repeat rows: 1-8.

Bind off as follows: After the last row 5, turn your work over; the Back Side: slip all the stitches from the left needle to the right one; now the working yarn is at the end of the row; turn your work over; the Front Side: slip 2 purlwise from the left needle to the right one, insert the left needle from left to right through the 1st slipped stitch and pass it over the 2nd stitch (now, there is 1 stitch on the right needle); *slip 1 purlwise from the left needle to the right one, insert the left needle from left to right through the 1st stitch on the right needle and pass it over the 2nd stitch (now, there is 1 stitch on the right needle)* repeat from * to * until the end of the row.

Note: For trimming, bind off loosely using larger needles than the working ones, in order to create a larger chain of edge stitches, as this type of binding off creates a tight chain of small edge stitches that look already finished.

Pattern 50

Cast on a multiple of 10, plus 2 for symmetry, and plus 2 edge stitches. Ten-stitch repeat. Repeat rows: 1-18. The edge stitches are not included in the description below and must be added. Slip the first edge stitch; purl the last edge stitch.

Knit through the back leg, purl as follows: with the working yarn in front of the stitch, insert the right needle through the stitch from back to front, then move the working yarn under the right needle and pull it through the stitch. The purl stitch that is worked this way sets up the knit stitch to be knitted through the back leg.

Description:

Row 1: *Purl 2, knit 4, slip the next 2 onto a cable needle in front of your work, knit the next 1, then knit the slipped 2, then knit the next 1* repeat from * to * until the end of the row before the edge stitch, purl 2.

Row 2: *Knit 2, purl 8* repeat from * to * until the end of the row before the edge stitch, knit 2.

Row 3: *Purl 2, knit 1, slip the next 1 onto a cable needle behind your work, knit the next 2, then knit the slipped 1, knit the next 1, slip 2 onto a cable needle in front of your work, knit the next 1, then knit the slipped 2* repeat from * to * until the end of the row before the edge stitch, purl 2.

Row 4: *Knit 2, purl 8* repeat from * to * until the end of the row before the edge stitch, knit 2.

Row 5: *Purl 2, slip 1 onto a cable needle behind your work, knit the next 2, then knit the slipped 1, knit the next 5* repeat from * to * until the end of the row before the edge stitch, purl 2.

Row 6: *Knit 2, purl 8* repeat from * to * until the end of the row before the edge stitch, knit 2.

Row 7: *Purl 2, knit 4, slip the next 2 onto a cable needle in front of your work, knit the next 1, then knit the slipped 2, knit the next 1* repeat from * to * until the end of the row before the edge stitch, purl 2.

Row 8: *Knit 2, purl 8* repeat from * to * until the end of the row before the edge stitch, knit 2.

Row 9: *Purl 2, knit 1, slip the next 1 onto a cable needle behind your work, knit the next 2, then knit the slipped 1, knit the next 1, slip the next 2 onto a cable needle in front of your work, knit the next 1, then knit the slipped 2* repeat from * to * until the end of the row before the edge stitch, purl 2.

Row 10: *Knit 2, purl 8* repeat from * to * until the end of the row before the edge stitch, knit 2.

Row 11: *Purl 2, slip the next 1 onto a cable needle behind your work, knit the next 2, then knit the slipped 1, knit the next 5* repeat from * to * until the end of the row before the edge stitch, purl 2.

Row 12: *Knit 2, purl 8* repeat from * to * until the end of the row before the edge stitch, knit 2.

Row 13: *Purl 2, knit 4, slip the next 2 onto a cable needle in front of your work, knit the next 1, then knit the slipped 2, knit the next 1* repeat from * to * until the end of the row before the edge stitch, purl 2.

Row 14: *Knit 2, purl 8* repeat from * to * until the end of the row before the edge stitch knit 2.

Row 15: *Purl 2, knit 1, slip the next 1 onto a cable needle behind your work, knit the next 2, then knit the slipped 1, knit the next 1, slip the next 2 onto a cable needle in front of your work, knit the next 1, then knit the slipped 2* repeat from * to * until the end of the row before the edge stitch, purl 2.

Row 16: *Knit 2, purl 8* repeat from * to * until the end of the row before the edge stitch, knit 2.

Row 17: *Purl 2, slip the next 1 onto a cable needle behind your work, knit the next 2, then knit the slipped 1, knit the next 5* repeat from * to * until the end of the row before the edge stitch, purl 2.

Row 18: *Knit 2, purl 8* repeat from * to * until the end of the row before the edge stitch, knit 2.

Repeat rows: 1-18.

Bind off as follows: After the last row 1, turn your work over; the Back Side: slip all the stitches from the left needle to the right one; now the working yarn is at the end of the row; turn your work over; the Front Side: slip 2 purlwise from the left needle to the right one, insert the left needle from left to right through the 1st slipped stitch and pass it over the 2nd stitch (now, there is 1 stitch on the right needle); *slip 1 purlwise from the left needle to the right one, insert the left needle from left to right through the 1st stitch on the right needle and pass it over the 2nd stitch (now, there is 1 stitch on the right needle)* repeat from * to * until the end of the row.

Note: For trimming, bind off loosely using larger needles than the working ones, in order to create a larger chain of edge stitches, as this type of binding off creates a tight chain of small edge stitches that look already finished.

About The Author

Internationally recognized hand knitwear designer Marina Molo has taught on various aspects of hand knitting over the past 30 years. In her book, *50 Shades of Stitches Vol. 3*, Marina Molo brings to life, in print, most popular knitting patterns, *Braids & Cables*, for all those who want to explore designing their own knitwear.

Visit the author's online store for unique items with knit prints, which include tank tops, leggings, tote bags, iphone cases, passport holders, luggage tags, wrapping paper, ribbons, pattern folders & much more at https://www.zazzle.com/store/shades_of_stitches or scan QR:

Marina Molo is currently working on several new publishing projects with SCR Media Inc.

Sign up to be notified when the next release is available at www.MarinaMolo.com.

What Do You Think of *50 Shades of Stitches*?

First of all, thank you for purchasing this book, 50 Shades of Stitches Volume 3.

I know you could have picked any other books to read, but you picked this book and for that I am extremely grateful. I hope that it adds value and quality to your everyday life. If so, it would be really nice if you could share this book with your friends and family by posting to [Facebook](#) and [Twitter](#).

*If you like this book and found some benefit in reading it, I'd like to hear from you and hope that you could take some time to post a review on Amazon. Your feedback and support will help the author to greatly improve her writing craft for future projects and make this book even better. Just type this link into your web browser **Getbook.at/Vol3** or scan code below:*

*I want you, the reader, to know that your review is very important and so, if you'd like to leave a review, all you have to do is copy into your web browser **Getbook.at/Vol3**.*

I wish you all the best in your future success!

www.ingramcontent.com/pod-product-compliance
Lightning Source LLC
Chambersburg PA
CBHW081458070526
44586CB00019B/2416